THE HUSBAND HANDBOOK

Jon —

A gift for you.

This book is the best advice I've seen lately on the subject of making a good marriage better

— Gordon   7/90

THE HUSBAND HANDBOOK

Essentials For Growing
A Successful Marriage

Dr. Bob Moorehead

Wolgemuth & Hyatt, Publishers, Inc.
Brentwood, Tennessee

The mission of Wolgemuth & Hyatt, Publishers, Inc. is to publish and distribute books that lead individuals toward:

- A personal faith in the one true God: Father, Son, and Holy Spirit;

- A lifestyle of practical discipleship; and

- A worldview that is consistent with the historic, Christian faith.

Moreover, the Company endeavors to accomplish this mission at a reasonable profit and in a manner which glorifies God and serves His Kingdom.

Unless otherwise noted, all scripture quotations are from the Holy Bible, New International Version. © 1973, 1978, 1984 International Bible Society. Used by permission of Zondervan Bible Publishers.

Wolgemuth & Hyatt, Publishers, Inc.
1749 Mallory Lane, Suite 110, Brentwood, Tennessee 37027

Library of Congress Cataloging-in-Publication Data

Moorehead, Bob.
   The husband handbook : essentials for growing a successful
marriage / Bob Moorehead. — 1st ed.
      p.   cm.
   ISBN 0-943497-43-4
   1. Husbands — Religious life. I. Title.
BV4846.m66 1990   90-30212
248.8'425 — dc20   CIP

These pages are dedicated to Glenita,
my wife of thirty-two years,
who has loved me in spite of my blemishes.

CONTENTS

INTRODUCTION

"Why is he picking on husbands? Isn't this the age of equality, and is it really legitimate to talk about marriage without talking about the wife as well as the husband?"

That's the question you men probably asked when you saw the title of this book, or when someone shoved it under your nose and said, "Here, read this. You need it!"

Well, you guys may as well know up front what my motives are in writing such a strange book. First of all, I am a husband. You need to know I'm not a perfect husband; I'm not even a good husband sometimes. My feet are made of clay just like yours, and I blow it again and again—just like you! So much of this book was written for *me*, believe it or not! I need the counsel of these pages far more than most of you who are holding this book in your hands.

Secondly, I happen to believe that it's the *husband* who is *ultimately* responsible for the success of his marriage. Yes, I know it takes two to make a marriage succeed, yet in God's pecking order, it's the male who is to shoulder the ultimate responsibility. In thirty-three years of counseling, I've discovered that in a majority of cases, marital difficulty and conflict can be traced right back to the man, though on the surface it may appear the problem is with both husband and wife.

Thirdly, this book is written because a national crisis exists in the home, the solution of which usually goes right back to the head of the household (or to the person who is supposed to be the head of the household), the husband.

Names have been changed in these pages to protect some husbands from being shot! But make no mistake, the situations are taken from real-life experiences.

Most Americans are suffering from an identity crisis today — they don't really know who they are. In my opinion, the segment that suffers most is husbands and prospective husbands, who don't have a clue as to what that role is supposed to include. We sometimes wonder why our society goes from bad to worse, and from worse to critical, and from critical to disastrous. The problem lies in the bedrock of our nation, the *home*. In the home, the root of the problem lies in the foundation and head, the husband.

The psalmist was right when he asked the question, "When the foundations are being destroyed, what can the righteous do?" (Psalms 11:3). I believe the husband is one of our foundation stones.

When the person who has been assigned the task of being the leader, the source, the bedrock of the home is out of alignment with God's purposes, everything tumbles like dominoes from there. Please know as you plow through these pages and stack your "husbandhood" against God's perfect model of husbandhood that I share with you those blatant deficiencies. Please see this as a handbook that has been dedicated to get you "back on track" with the most important task you have in the world if you're married — *being God's kind of husband to your wife! It will make a big difference in your life . . . and hers.*

Bob Moorehead

1

KNOWING
THE DIFFERENCE

In my experience, at least 30 percent of all marriage breakups could be avoided if the man just knew the difference between male and female.

There *is* a difference, just in case you haven't noticed!

No, I'm not talking about the physical differences — you've had no problem discovering what those are. The problem is, in fact, that most males enter marriage blindly assuming that physical differences are the *only* differences. That's not only an erroneous assumption, it's a disastrous assumption, as some of you reading this have discovered.

&ã&   &ã&   &ã&

The wedding was one of the most beautiful I had ever seen. Rick and Denise could have qualified for the "All-American Couple." Rick was extremely handsome, tall, with thick black hair, a masculine model all the way. I watched his flashing eyes as Denise's father walked her down the aisle. You could see why his eyes were flashing when you looked at her. A picture of pure femininity, Denise walked gracefully in a beautiful wedding dress with a white satin hat covering the top of her long, naturally curly, dark brown hair.

All you could hear at the reception were the words, "What a beautiful couple!" And it was true. I watched as this young couple left for their honeymoon in Canada — they were so in love.

You can imagine my surprise three months later to see that Rick had made an appointment to see me. When he walked into my office, what a different man from the one I had seen on that wedding day. With drooping shoulders, hair out of place, he didn't need to say a word; I could see the frustration on his face. "I'm embarrassed to come see you and take your time, but . . . well . . . uh . . . well, there's no easy way to say it. . . . If I had known women were like this, I would have never married." He proceeded to tell me how their first argument began only one hour out of town, and how from day one she seemed to be so stubborn, so unreasonable, and so moody. The relationship had gone from piping hot to lukewarm to subzero!

I listened for about thirty minutes as Rick related episode after episode. Soon I picked up a pattern and knew the problem. Interrupting him, I said, "Rick, did you know there is a difference between men and women?" His response was quick. "Yes, I know that. That's why I got married!"

I soon discovered Rick's knowledge of the *difference* was only skin-deep. Denise was very attractive physically, and Rick had fallen in love with her body, her voice, her eyes, but did not realize he was taking on as a life's partner a creature radically different from himself, both emotionally and socially. I'm glad to report that after a few tense times and several counseling sessions, Rick and Denise are doing well, but only after he began to learn the differences between men and women.

ঌ   ঌ   ঌ

Husband, have you found yourself saying things like: "I don't understand my wife!" "I don't know what she wants!" "I can't figure out why she changes her mind so much." "Now what have I done wrong?" "She doesn't seem to like any gifts I buy her." "Our lives just aren't 'meshing' together."

Maybe you can add a few. I believe the first requirement for any man before marrying is to make sure he understands, at least to some degree, what makes a woman tick, what are the ingredients that make her who she is, and why he and she keep passing each other on opposite tracks. What are the differences? Take note! Listen up! Get it straight!

Dependent and Independent

Generally speaking, men are independent creatures. They are not prone to emotionally lean and depend on others but are designed to be strong posts on which the female leans. Remember, it was out of the man God took the material to create the woman. Most men are self-starters. On the other hand, women are created to be dependent. In spite of what we're told and read in papers and magazines, many females depend upon the male for support, encouragement, confirmation, and sometimes direction.

So, fellows, when you can't understand why your wife isn't a stronger person, or a person who takes the bull by the horns more often, just remember she was not designed to be the aggressive one with an independent spirit. Remember the words of Peter: "Treat them with respect as the *weaker* partner" (1 Peter 3:7, emphasis added). Oh, by the way, guys, if she is the "weaker" sex — guess who the "weak" sex is?

Two Sources of Fulfillment

Another deep difference between men and women lies in where they find their greatest fulfillment.

Fulfillment for most women doesn't come from going toe-to-toe with the business world in a competitive way, nor is it found in achieving, exceeding sales quotas, or "winning the contract." Men are usually fulfilled by their jobs. Much of their identity comes from where they work, while a woman's fulfillment and identity comes from her husband, her family, her home, and perhaps some hobbies. Remember, guys, one is not more important than or superior to the other, but they are different.

So, when your wife isn't ecstatic over your promotion or the fact you were salesman of the month, or isn't too conversant about hardware and software, don't think you're being rejected. She's just coming from another mindset than the one you have.

Two Levels of Energy

Not only because they are built more delicately, but also because of their general make-up, many women do not have the energy level of most men. Some guys can come home after eight hours of work and catch a match of tennis, a round of golf, a four-mile jog, or a workout at the health club. In contrast, many women after struggling with the house, the kids, the phone, the laundry, and the stove all day are on the way to exhaustion by 6:00 P.M.

So, men, when your wife doesn't seem all that excited about doing something with you late in the day, remember her level of energy may be running much lower than yours. It's not lack of interest on her part; it's lack of horsepower! Generally, a woman's energy tank is depleted much faster than most men. Her weariness by 8:00 at night is both physical and emotional.

Two Views of Beauty

A structural steel engineer took his wife faithfully to the concrete and steel skyscraper under construction. Two or three times a week, they would drive over, and he would ooh and aah, pointing out the symmetry of the beams, the enormity of the foundation, the mathematical formulas that made thirty-eight floors possible. He couldn't understand why she nearly fell asleep. Why wasn't she interested? Simple. Men see beauty in different things from women. In every marriage husbands must remember this basic difference to keep interests balanced.

When buying a new car, for example, the male is excited about its horsepower, its braking system, its rack-and-pinion steering, its electronic ignition, and its gas mileage. On the other hand, the woman is excited about its upholstery, its color, and the sound of its radio! She could care less whether it is a four-cylinder, eight-cylinder, or whether or not it even has cylinders!

So, men, remember what things your wife deems beautiful. A beautifully arranged bouquet of flowers is a work of art to her, while a rebuilt water pump you've installed that works is beautiful to you.

Decision Making: Reason or Emotion

Men, if you haven't discovered it yet, women are *emotional* human beings.

One man recently told me his wife wanted to buy life insurance from a salesman because he was a young man trying to earn money to feed his four kids and wife. She was ready to make a decision of fifty thousand dollars worth of life insurance because of the salesman's circumstances, not because it was a good deal. Now, that's not necessarily bad in and of itself, but it is a different basis from the basis on which a man would decide.

One couple told me they looked at a home to buy that had a view of Mt. Ranier. It was thirty thousand dollars higher than the other home down the street, which had just as much square footage. The wife wanted to buy the home with the view; the husband wanted to buy the home down the street. She enjoyed the view, an emotional enjoyment. He wanted to enjoy the monthly payments, a practical preference. He was thinking practically while she was thinking aesthetically. See the difference? Again, one basis isn't superior to another; they're just different, radically different.

A husband should not insist his wife make all her decisions on a rational basis. Don't try to remake her in your image!

Parrot and Clam

Another basic difference between most men and women is that men don't talk much to their wives, and women tend to talk to their husbands excessively. A common complaint I hear is, "He won't express his emotions; he won't open up and speak his mind; he doesn't communicate with me." Few men say, "Honey, let's go for a walk and just talk a while." Some guys come in from the battlefield every night, overeat, plop in the chair, turn on the tube, snooze off and on, then wobble off to bed. Very little communication—very little talking with their spouse.

God has given women the ability to talk out their deep inner feelings. Men, on the other hand, tend to keep their true feelings deep inside. There is a mind-set among most men, not all, that says it's wimpy to talk to your wife about anything except the necessities—"What's for dinner?" "How much did it cost?" "Can we make love?" and "Can you get me something cold to drink?"

Husbands, learn to talk on a level that's deeper than the bare necessities. How long has it been since you came home from work and said, "How did your day go? Did you know I was praying for you today? Is there anything I can help you with tonight?"

Sexual Needs

Men and women are different here, as you know! Men are action oriented, and women are emotionally ori-

ented. The height of thrill for a man is sexual inter-
course and the climax. He arrives at that much more
quickly than a woman.

Intimacy for a man happens in bed, usually very
quickly. For a woman it begins in the kitchen with a
hug, a squeeze, a pat, soft words of love spoken. Simply knowing her husband loves her and holds her can
be as exhilarating as reaching an orgasm for a woman.
That doesn't mean sex isn't important for the woman,
but it's not always the great highlight that it is for the
man. Women, obviously, are not built to become sexually excited on the spur of the moment. The man is.
This calls for great balance, great sensitivity.

Men, remember, if you love your wife like Christ
loved the church (and those are our instructions, see
Ephesians 5:25), you will honor her uniqueness in this
sensitive area. Remember Rick? Part of his problem
was that he didn't understand why he couldn't come
home from work and in five minutes go right to bed
with his wife, and why she wouldn't be very excited
about his body. Once he learned that women are
aroused slowly, they enjoyed a wonderful sex life — before that, however, it was World War III. Many men
really believe their wives are frigid, when in fact a
woman's feelings don't shift gears in three minutes.

Doing Versus Being

Men are "doers" while women are basically "be-ers."
That is not to imply that women are lazy, lethargic, or

slow. It is to say that most women have an easier time being passive than most men. One psychologist defined husband and wife as *aggressor/reactor.* Obviously, there are some exceptions to that. But it's generally true, for example, that a man would rather work in a workshop than read a book. He'd rather saw down a tree than water the lawn. His is a more active nature, and many a marriage has been written off as incompatible because both spouses didn't realize this basic difference. That's why most men don't like to go window-shopping. Most men see strolling past displays in windows as a total waste of time, because nothing is being accomplished. That's why most men on an automobile trip feel the need to cover eight hundred miles per day, while the wife would like to cover about three hundred and sightsee the rest of the time.

Fellows, recognize that women are different from men. Thank God for that — and adapt! You'll be much happier.

Once you recognize these basic differences, your relationship with your wife will go much smoother. Rick's did!

2

BE WHAT YOU ARE, MR. LEADER!

The coach's razzle-dazzle plays weren't gaining any yardage, and his team was down twenty to three! It was the fourth quarter with eight minutes remaining on the clock. The coach sent the word in to the quarterback, "Give the ball to Leroy!" Next play: the ball is snapped, the quarterback keeps the ball, runs around the tight end, and loses three yards! The coach sends in the word again, this time with more authority, "Give the ball to Leroy!" Again, the ball is snapped; the quarterback tries the quarterback sneak. He's creamed! This time, the coach calls the quarterback over to the sidelines. "What's wrong with you? Don't you understand English? I said, Give the ball to Leroy!" The quarterback responded, "Leroy says he don't *want* the ball!"

I can identify with Leroy. With four 285-pound, mean-looking tackles determined to decimate anybody holding a football, I agree with Leroy—I don't think I would want the ball either! But let's face hard facts. If Leroy is touted as being the select carrier by the coach, he must take the ball and run with it—or his team will lose the game. He must *take* the ball, like it or not! Do you get my drift?

Men, when it comes to marriage, like it or not, dangerous or not, convenient or not, the Head Coach has designated us to take the ball and run with it. Failure to do so could mean losing the game of marriage! Today millions of well-meaning men have abrogated their headship in marriage. Like a large ship—whose rudder is missing—wanders aimlessly over rough waters, so many marriages aimlessly drift over rough waters in whatever direction the wind is blowing. Most of them head for the fatal reefs where they're broken up!

God's earliest description of the man is a description of authority: "Let us make man in our image, in our likeness, and let them rule over the fish of the sea and the birds of the air, over the livestock, over all the earth, and over all the creatures that move along the ground" (Genesis 1:26).

In Genesis 2:7 we're told that the very breath of God has been breathed into us! In Genesis 2:15 we're told that God put man in the garden of Eden to work it and take care of it. He was in charge, in authority. Further in that chapter, He gave man the awesome responsibility of naming all the creatures. Later, God caused man to take a deep nap, and while he was asleep, He took from man that marvelous creation, woman.

Men, that was a successful and wonderful surgery. When Adam looked at her, he was awed and said, "This is now bone of my bones and flesh of my flesh" (Genesis 2:23). In our vernacular, "Wow, I can't believe this beautiful creation came out of me!"

Even after Adam and Eve fell in sin, God made it clear what the marriage relationship was to be: "To the woman he said, 'I will greatly increase your pains in childbearing; with pain you will give birth to children. Your desire will be for your husband, and he will *rule over you*'" (Genesis 3:16, emphasis added).

It's evident that the male in marriage is the leader, the general manager, the CEO, if you please, of the marriage. Before you get puffed up with pride, seeing this as some masculine privilege, let me assure you that whatever part of it is privilege, there is more that is responsibility and obligation.

Terri was in tears when she cornered me in the hallway. A wife for the past sixteen years, she was frustrated, exasperated, and totally discouraged. "All I want Ken to do," she forced out, "is lead. I have to be mother, decision maker, financier, determiner, and the one at every meal to say grace. If only he would lead!" Terri was expressing what so many women have told me in recent years. They want their husbands to lead, they desire their husbands to lead, they pray for their

husbands to lead! Believe it or not, with few exceptions, most wives cry out for their husbands to be the
leader in their marriage.

Where that doesn't happen, a reversal of God's
order enters the marriage, and the seeds of destruction
are sown; the harvest being not very far behind!

Let's take a deeper look at that interesting phrase
written for the sake of all husbands in 1 Peter: "Husbands, in the same way be considerate as you live with
your wives, and treat them with respect as the weaker
partner" (3:7). Peter calls the wife a *weaker* partner.
Again, if she is a *weaker* partner, what does that make
the husband? You guessed it — a *weak* partner. So,
men, we are not invincible, infallible, nor are we Mr.
Strong all the time. Even though we are the weak partner and our wives are the weaker partners, this verse
implies, and rightly so, that husbands are still called to
be the leaders in the marriage.

Paul confirms this in his writings. He says to the
wives: "Wives, submit to your husbands as to the
Lord. For the husband is the head of the wife as Christ
is the head of the church" (Ephesians 5:22–23). God
never created anything or anyone without an order.
Marriage is no exception. He has placed the male in
the position of leadership (not dictatorship) and desires
to affect the whole family through him.

Again, before you swell with pride, be awed with
the responsibility on your shoulders.

Now, what is your role as leader? It's clearly spelled out for you in that same chapter of Ephesians. You have one major responsibility as leader in your marriage: "Husbands, *love your wives, just as Christ loved the church* and gave himself up for her" (Ephesians 5:25, emphasis added).

That one major responsibility, like a diamond, has many facets. Remember, the one command is: *Love your wife like Christ loves the church.* If you're going to carry that out, you need to know how Christ loves the church.

A Purifying Love

A man recently demonstrated a water purification system. He showed me the secret to the whole thing. Tap water is forced through a filter which changes the water from hard to soft, from impure to pure. Husbands were designed on God's drafting board to be filters that purify.

If we're going to love our wives like Christ loved the church, then remember, one of the ways He loved the church was by giving Himself "up for her to make her holy, cleansing her by the washing with water through the word" (Ephesians 5:25–26).

That's a big order, but a possible one. Your wife's purity, holiness, and godliness is *your* responsibility, not the pastor's, not the books she's reading, not her Bible study, but yours! Now before you panic, let me encourage you. It's not as hard as you might think. In fact, it's quite simple. Her purity before God will flow from *your* purity before Him.

This means there is no place for impurity in your life! Let's start with the worst. There's no place for developing a relationship with the woman where you work. She may be your secretary, and you may feel attracted to her, but run before it's too late. In fact, you have a responsibility to change jobs if you can't control the lust. You may be saying, "I would never have an affair with another woman." Yet, you will see R and X rated movies when the opportunity comes; you may even skim through the Playboy and Hustler magazines when traveling, or worse, watch the skin flicks in your hotel room. You abrogate your leadership when you succumb to such things.

If you're serious about doing this God's way, all filth must go. A clean wife will happen only by the example of a clean husband. A helpful word, men: The only way you can stay clean is to get into God's Word on a daily basis, and let it lodge in your heart. Without it, you are a sitting duck for sexual sins especially. The psalmist said: "I have hidden your word in my heart that I might not sin against you" (Psalms 119:11).

A Beautifying Love

A wife is not made beautiful by the dress shop or the beautician, but by her husband. Loving your wife like

Christ loves the church means it's a beautifying love. Ephesians 5 goes on to say: "To present her to himself as a radiant church, without stain or wrinkle or any other blemish" (v. 27). When a man recently said to me, "My wife isn't beautiful anymore," I responded, "She is the extension of what you've made her." You are the best "wrinkle remover" she'll ever have.

How do you beautify your wife? By enabling her to live a worry-free life. You do it by removing those things that could bring stress, worry, or fear to her. This means holding her often and letting her know verbally how committed you are to her.

A Nourishing Love

Part of the package of loving your wife like Christ loved the church is to provide the proper nourishment for her. In Ephesians 5:29, Paul said, "After all, no one ever hated his own body, but he feeds and cares for it, just as Christ does the church." I was sharing this principle in a men's conference in the Midwest. After the session, one of the men said to me, "I nourish my wife . . . have you seen her lately? She doesn't look like she's missed too many meals!" He missed my point, obviously. Of course we're to provide physical food for our wives, but more importantly we're to provide spiritual food for them. That doesn't mean you're to come home from work, get out your big Bible, and say, "All right, sit down. It's time for me to teach you the Word of God!" The minute you're arrogant about your spiritual headship you've disqualified yourself to lead.

But make no mistake about it, one of the greatest things your wife can ever see you doing is reading the Word and then sharing with her the new insights of what you've read. How long has it been, for example, since you said to your wife, "Honey, let me share with you this Scripture I've been memorizing," or "Honey, in my quiet time this morning, the Lord led me to this verse of Scripture." No, you don't have to get super spiritual, just let her know you take your relationship with Jesus Christ seriously. Most husbands give no evidence whatsoever to their mates that they have even cracked the Bible in weeks.

As the high priest of your home, you're to be the spiritual leader, not the spiritual follower. In many marriages where both partners are believers, it's the wife who is on the cutting spiritual edge, not the husband. This doesn't mean you have to be the resident Bible scholar, but it does mean that you're the one who initiates reading the Word and praying together, and that you lead the way in going to church and Christian seminars. Be what you are meant to be — the spiritual leader who nourishes your wife.

A Caring Love

Paul says in verse 29 of Ephesians 5 that you're to not only feed your wife but care for her. This means letting her know where she stands in your priorities. Ask yourself, "What have I done in the last week to show my wife I love her? How about the last month? How about the last three months?"

The one thing a wife cannot survive long without is the evidence that she is very high on her husband's scale of priorities. Where is she in your "pecking order" of priorities?

A Uniting Love

"For this reason a man will leave his father and mother and be united to his wife, and the two will become one flesh" (Ephesians 5:31). Leaving and cleaving — that's your assignment! What does it mean to be "united" to your wife? Does it mean you have lost all individuality — it's all been blended into her? Not exactly! It does mean that you need to be a part of her life, her feelings; to be sensitive to her needs, her emotions, her reactions.

When was the last time you asked your wife, "Honey, how did your day go today?" "How are you doing with that dress you're sewing?" "How was your workout at the health club today?" You care because you're part of her.

Men, don't forget, you've been thrown the ball! You're the God-ordained leader and head of your marriage and family. You can't abrogate or delegate that responsibility to someone else, or stick your head in the sand and pretend it will go away. God's chain of command is clear: "Now I want you to realize that the head of every man is Christ, and the head of the woman is man, and the head of Christ is God" (1 Corinthians 11:3). Christ is your head, and you are your wife's head; this is God's order, and it can't be improved on.

Here's a test for you. After each statement circle the one who primarily does the task.

1. Calls neighbor about barking dog.   *Wife* or *Husband*

2. Calls mortgage company about late payment.   *Wife* or *Husband*

3. Awards contract to house painter.   *Wife* or *Husband*

4. Sees that children do their homework.   *Wife* or *Husband*

5. Makes final decisions on child's social life.   *Wife* or *Husband*

6. Gets estimates on broken dishwasher.   *Wife* or *Husband*

7. Sees that yard is kept up in summer.   *Wife* or *Husband*

8. Initiates a savings program for the family.   *Wife* or *Husband*

9. Makes final decision on   *Wife* or *Husband*
    financing the new car.

10. Initiates frequency of   *Wife* or *Husband*
    church attendance.

Who does most of those things? If seven out of ten are done by your wife, men, you have abrogated some leadership and initiative in the home. Remember, your wife wants you to lead, not dictate, and to show some determination and direction for the marriage and the family.

Someone gave me a poster with a bunch of ducks walking in a park, and it says: "Lead, follow, or get out of the way." That's what a lot of wives could easily say to their husbands. We need to change all of that.

Leroy may abrogate his responsibility on the gridiron, but you dare not. Be what you are, Mr. Leader, and *lead*.

3

GET THOSE PRIORITIES STRAIGHT!

R andy sat across from my desk, looked me squarely in the eye, and said; "I've been burning the candle at both ends, and I'm here for more wax!" Randy's real problem lay in the fact that his marriage of eight years was coming unglued. Renee, his wife, normally a warm, loving, cheerful woman, had become distant, morose, somewhat cold, and unresponsive. The biggest thing Randy had going for him in this situation was that he was aware something wasn't right. That's more than can be said for many husbands who purr right along and never notice a thing.

After only thirty minutes, the obvious was clear. Randy, like so many males in their early thirties, had his priorities confused. His sales job was demanding close to sixty hours per week, which included being gone one or two evenings every week. On top of that

he played at least a couple of racquetball games a
week with his boss, was on the board of his civic club,
was serving as president of his homeowners' associa-
tion, played basketball on the church league early Saturday mornings, and was taking one night course at the
City Community College. No wonder his candle was
about out! It wasn't more wax he needed; it was a re-
turn to sane priorities.

Randy and I got a piece of notebook paper and
numbered one to five. Then I asked him to list in se-
quential order his current scale of priorities. This is
what he wrote:

1. Job

2. Sports (both watching and playing)

3. Jesus Christ

4. Wife

5. Civic club and further schooling

I took another piece of paper, numbered it one to
five, and wrote the following:

1. Jesus Christ

2. *Wife*

3. Job

4. Church activities

5. Hobbies, sports, and civic clubs, etc.

For a minute I thought Randy would have a coronary! (Maybe you are feeling chest pains too about now.) The fact is, however, the second list of priorities is absolutely essential if a man's marriage is going to survive, to say nothing about flourishing.

All of this is predicated upon that very important section of Scripture. "Husbands, in the same way be considerate as you live with your wives, and treat them with respect as the weaker partner and as heirs with you of the gracious gift of life, so that nothing will hinder your prayers" (1 Peter 3:7). Next to your commitment to Jesus Christ, comes your wife, not your career, not your hobbies, not your exercise program, not your parents, not your children, but your *wife!*

Peter starts out by telling husbands to be considerate. That word means fair, to acknowledge fairly her place in our scale of values.

Peter then says, "as you *live* with your wives." That doesn't just mean you both share the same address, eat at the same table, have a joint checking account, and sleep in the same bed; it goes deeper than all that. The word *with* in this context means dwelling with in close proximity, both physically and emotionally. Move in the same direction that she moves. Get on board with her, and let her know that you're a part of her team, not some other team.

Then he says, "Treat them with respect." Other versions say "honor" them. In your own mind and heart accord her the rightful place in your priorities, and let her know where she stands in your scale of values!

I've learned in thirty-two years of counseling that there are many things a wife *can* live without if necessary. She *can* live without adequate money, clothes, even without physical sex, if she has to for awhile. She can live without a nice house, jewelry, up-to-date appliances, her own car, and nice vacations. *But the one thing she cannot live without is not knowing where she stands in her husband's scale of values!* Or worse, *knowing* that she is third, fourth, fifth, or sixth on his list!

Men, your wife was not made by God to survive not being sure how vital, valuable, precious, and essential she is to you.

Maybe by now you're wondering, "Does my wife really know she's right up at the top on my list?" Here's a good test to take. Circle either *yes* or *no.*

- Does the amount of time I spend   *Yes No*
  with her convey that she's at the
  top of my list?

- Do I tell her I love her at times   *Yes No*
  other than sex?

- If I had a free ticket to a Super   *Yes No*
  Bowl game and it was on our anniversary, would I stay with her
  rather than go to the game?

- Do I personally buy her things at   *Yes   No*
  times other than Christmas, birth-
  day, and anniversary?

- Do I ever take the initiative in hav-   *Yes   No*
  ing her be with her parents?

- Do I ask daily, "How did your day   *Yes   No*
  go today?"

- Does she know I highly value her   *Yes   No*
  opinion?

- Does she know I listen when she   *Yes   No*
  talks?

- Would I rather be with her alone at   *Yes   No*
  a restaurant than with her and other
  friends?

- Does she buy clothes for herself at   *Yes   No*
  my urging?

- Do I ever leave her a love note?   *Yes   No*

Well, how did you do? If half of them are checked "no," your wife isn't high enough on your priority list. Paul said in 1 Corinthians 7:33 that a married man is concerned with how to please his wife. That's the bottom line. Are you living in your marriage with the idea of what's in it for you? If you are, you're in for a great disappointment. Selfish expectations in marriage are never met. If you're thinking, *"I expect my wife to cook my meals, launder my clothes, clean my house, gratify my sex drive, raise my children, and stay slim and beautiful,"* you're concentrating on the wrong things. On the other hand, if you're thinking, *"I wonder how I can satisfy her, fulfill her, make her happy, and make her look good in the eyes of others,"* then you're thinking right.

Peter says that wives are "heirs with you of the gracious gift of life" (1 Peter 3:7). Do you recognize her as a child of God, as your sister in the Lord? Do you honor her as one of God's children, precious and valuable to God? If so, then part of your responsibility to her is to let her know from time to time how precious she is according to the Bible.

Sometimes I leave a love note for my wife in the mornings when I have to leave very early, and at the bottom I write *Proverbs 31:10-11.* Know what those verses say?

> A wife of noble character who can find?
> She is worth far more than rubies.
> Her husband has full confidence in her
> and lacks nothing of value.

These verses from Proverbs bring a great sense of the right kind of esteem to a wife and powerfully let her know how much you believe in God's Word and that you're applying that Word to her life. She will be thrilled that you would even think of her with verses like that.

Now back to 1 Peter—he ends verse 7 with a rationale for all his advice: "so that nothing will hinder your prayers." A husband's spiritual relationship to the Lord is affected directly by how much he values his wife! A man's spiritual life will go flat very quickly when he's out of harmony with his wife, especially when he leaves her to wonder where she stands in his value system.

Since most men are pragmatists, maybe you're asking: "Tell me, what can I practically do to let my wife know she's the most important and most vital person in my life?" You asked for it, so here's a list. Pick and choose from the list what seems good for you to do. (What can you add to this list?)

- Bring flowers at least once a month.

- Leave a love note where she'll find it while you're at work.

- Initiate a trip for her to go see her parents.

- Arrange in advance baby-sitting so you can take her out.

- Let her know you're praying for her daily.

- Pray for her when she's the least bit ill.

- Mail her a thank-you note occasionally, just thanking her for being your wife and letting her know she counts!

- Plan a surprise overnight trip for her at a nice place.

- Plan a night to keep the kids, give her some money, and tell her to go shopping and to take her time.

- Give her a neck and back massage when she doesn't ask for it in a setting not designed for sex.

- Clean the table off and send her to the den to relax and read the paper.

- Offer to call her parents long distance so she can talk.

- Surprise her occasionally with a gift certificate to a beauty salon.

- Pray for her and thank God for her out loud at mealtime.

- Call her from work to tell her you're bringing dinner home tonight.

Remember Randy? He felt he was losing Renee. He swallowed hard, looked at the rearranged list I wrote for him, and decided to try it. I noticed in only a few weeks a new smile on Renee's face, a lilt in her walk, and an unfurrowed brow on Randy's face.

Men, if your wife seems distant, cold, unresponsive, and disinterested in you, take a hard look at the you she's not responding to, and do something about it. Get her up from fourth, fifth, or sixth place on your list to the top, just under Jesus Christ. *You'll change her life . . . and yours.*

Mazie V. Caruthers said it best in this prayer we men need to pray about our wives:

Prayer of Any Husband

Lord, may there be no moment in her life
When she regrets that she became my wife,
And keep her dear eyes just a trifle blind
To my defects, and to my failings kind!

Help me to do the utmost that I can
To prove myself her measure of a man,
But if I fail, as mortals may,
Grant that she never sees my feet of clay!

And let her make allowance, now and then,
That we are only grown-up boys, we men,
So, loving all her children, she will see,
Sometimes, a remnant of the child in me!

Since years must bring to all their load of care,
Let us together every burden bear,
And when Death beckons one its path along,
May not the two of us be parted long.

(From *Masterpieces of Religious
Verse*, Harper Brothers, Publishers,
1948.)

4

WHEN VEXED
OVER SEX

With only two years of marriage under his belt, Larry was frustrated, to say the least. He had married at twenty-two years old, young by some standards, but he and Beth seemed fairly mature. Larry was a man of few words. As he sat across my desk with a sheepish grin, he got straight to the point when I asked how I could help him.

"Well, it's sex! I want it and she doesn't!" That was it. Short, simple, straight to the issue. We talked, but the further I got, guess who had the problem, he or Beth? You guessed it! It was Larry. You might be interested in knowing that in cases of sexual incompatibility, most of the time, the husband is the primary culprit. A lack of sensitivity coupled with inadequate knowledge of how a woman is emotionally made put him at a disadvantage.

Though most men don't like to hear that, it goes back to the premise that the male, the husband is ultimately responsible for the success of his marriage. After all, he is the leader, the head, the high priest, the general manager. Therefore, he must understand God's perspective and original design for sex in marriage.

Purposes of Sex

God created sex. He designed it and intricately built it into every person. We need to answer the question — what is the purpose of sex in marriage?

Sex Is for Human Reproduction

Has it ever dawned on you that God could have made other arrangements for reproduction? The possible methods are limitless if you'll let your imagination run wild. The fact is, however, He chose sex as the experience in which human conception takes place. "So God created man in his own image, in the image of God he created him; male and female he created them. God blessed them and said to them, 'Be fruitful and increase in number; fill the earth, and subdue it'" (Genesis 1:27-28). Having children is not only a good idea, but also it's a command of God. Coitus is the loving act by which conception takes place.

Many men become very selfish at this point and want all their wife's attention to focus on them; thus the thought of children becomes a threat to a man. Perish the thought! God doesn't specify how many children you're supposed to have—there are many factors that might determine that—but that we *are* to have children is clearly commanded. Exceptions occur when there is physical inability or some form of infertility that may be irreversible. Even then, adoption can take place.

Sex brings about children, and God expresses the value we're to place on those children. "Sons are a heritage from the LORD, children a reward from him. Like arrows in the hands of a warrior are sons born in one's youth. Blessed is the man whose quiver is full of them" (Psalms 127:3-5). Note, children are a *reward.* They are never to be considered as a punishment. Sex is not the reward. The result of that loving act—children—becomes the reward.

Sex Is for Close, Personal Companionship

After God created man, He looked upon him, and saw him as an incomplete being, then said, "It is not good for the man to be alone. I will make a helper suitable for him" (Genesis 2:18).

Can you imagine how lonely man was? Can you imagine the deep need for companionship in Adam when God spoke these words? Can you imagine Adam's pleasure the first time he saw the lovely being God formed out of his side? He might well have thought and said, "Wow! I knew there was something missing all along!"

The male is completed by the female; they are companions. Marriage itself is a venture in interdependence as two people sail rough seas. "In the Lord, however, woman is not independent of man, nor is man independent of woman" (1 Corinthians 11:11). This close companionship can reach its apex, its summit in the sex act where two individuals become one flesh, the physical expression of their completeness. Biblically, this is done exclusively within the confines of marriage.

Sex Is for Romantic Pleasure

Some think it is almost sacrilegious to say that sex is for pleasure, but it's true. When God created sex, part of His design was that both man and wife would be deeply pleasured. For people raised in an "ultra-prudish" family, this truth comes hard. The myth that somehow sex in marriage is a "chore" and "dirty" hasn't died easily, even in this loose generation, and afflicts the male as well as the female. I urge every man to read Song of Solomon, especially chapter 7:1-9. There, Solomon describes his wife, and in every breath there is the heartbeat of pleasure. Men, you need to learn how to verbalize your affections as you sexually appreciate your wife.

The Bible is clear on the responsibility of the husband toward his wife: "But since there is so much immorality, each man should have his own wife, and each woman her own husband" (1 Corinthians 7:2).

Our sexual needs and desires were placed in us by God; thus the means for their fulfillment was arranged for as well. That fulfillment comes as we give ourselves sexually to our wives as lovers.

Healthy Sexual Guidelines

Having understood the purpose of sex in marriage, we now need to understand the "guidelines" for husbands to enable them to nurture a healthy sexual relationship between them and their spouses.

Have the Right Motive for Sex

A man once said to me, "I have a right to have my sexual needs met in my marriage, don't I?" Where was that man's emphasis? It was totally on himself, his gratification, his pleasure, his fulfillment. Sorry, but that's the wrong emphasis in sex. The man's emphasis must be on pleasing and pleasuring his wife, not himself. If that's done properly and in that order, he will end up extremely pleased. A major part of his pleasure is in knowing she is pleased! Notice how the Bible bears this out: "The husband should fulfill his marital duty to his wife" (1 Corinthians 7:3).

Notice the word *duty*. Now I grant you that sex in marriage is more than duty, but it is a duty we men have. What is that duty? It is to please her! Paul goes on to say in that chapter: "But a married man is concerned about the affairs of this world—*how he can please his wife*" (1 Corinthians 7:33, emphasis added). Paul is reminding his readers that in marriage, the primary concern for the man is learning how he can please his wife, not himself.

It's interesting that when you read the husband's responsibilities in marriage in Ephesians 5, you read nothing about his demanding his rights. You only read about his responsibilities. That's true in sex. If your primary concern in having sex with your wife is how you will be "relieved and gratified," you are prostituting the sex act in marriage. I believe that is partly what the writer was talking about in Hebrews 13:4 when he speaks of keeping the marriage bed pure. A man can defile his marriage bed in ways other than adultery. One of those ways is having self-gratification as your sole motive.

Start Yesterday

To start yesterday sounds strange, but understanding the emotional differences between male and female, a husband will be wise to begin his lovemaking sexually in the kitchen and not the bedroom. It may culminate in bed, but it often begins while your wife is standing in front of the sink or the kitchen stove. It may start with a phone call from you at work. It begins with loving words, then moves to loving acts of being helpful. It continues with questions of concern like, "How was your day today?" "How's your gardening project coming?" It moves on from there to speaking affectionate words. Many American husbands only tell their wives they love them in bed just prior to or during the sex act! Those words need to be spoken in the car, the kitchen, the hallway, the porch, or in the yard long before they're spoken in bed. This way, lovemaking in bed is simply the continuation of a basic attitude that began yesterday, or at least a few hours earlier in other parts of the home!

Remember, a woman is not instantly aroused; lovemaking is a process and the husband should prove to his wife that she is more to him than merely a sex object. She is the most priceless person in his life.

Avoid Society's Expectations

I read of a man who went to a marriage counselor complaining that he wasn't "getting" enough sex from his wife. He said, "Do you know how many times a week the average American couple has sex?" The counselor didn't have a clue.

The man's voice rose, "Two and seven-tenths times, that's how many! And I'm only getting it two and two-tenths times."

I realize that's an extreme and probably greatly embellished, but the principle is there. Many men think because of what they read or hear that there is a "right" number of times they're to have sex with their wives. They're allowing what they read or hear to literally run (and ruin) their sex life. Once a man in his thirties said to me, "People our age ought to be having sex at least five times per week, and I'm lucky if I get it five times per month!" My only response to him was, "Who said?" Other men read of weird and kinky ways couples have sex, then get upset because they think they're missing out. Unrealistic expectations— avoid them like the plague. What's natural for you? Who's counting anyway? Sex between a married couple is private, personal, and not to be talked about with others. What is fulfilling for both is the right expectation, regardless of frequency or method!

Eliminate "Routineness" in Sex

Part of the mystique of sex is the spontaneity of it all. To put it on the calendar is to miss it entirely. To confine it to the same day of the week, same time of night, same words, same approach, same things beforehand, same things afterward becomes humdrum. No one would think of eating hamburgers at every meal in the same place at the same time, all the time. If it's all predictable, it has lost its meaning and its depth. Be creative with your wife.

Set Parameters for Your Affections

What are those parameters? Sex is confined to your wife! Arousal is confined to her! Nothing will damage and cripple marital sex more than an extramarital sexual affair. Apart from being un-Biblical and ungodly, it

violates something most precious in your wife, a sense
of fidelity and tenderness.

Listen to what a wise sage said in Scripture:

> Drink water from your own cistern, running water
> from your own well. Should your springs overflow
> in the streets, your streams of water in the public
> squares? Let them be yours alone, never to be
> shared with strangers. May your fountain be
> blessed, and may you rejoice in the wife of your
> youth. A loving doe, a graceful deer — may *her*
> breasts satisfy you always, may you ever be capti-
> vated by *her* love. (Proverbs 5:15-19, emphasis
> added)

Those are strong words. In short, they tell married
men to confine their romantic love and the arousal for
that love to their wives.

How saddened I was to hear a wife divulge that her
husband had to spend ten or fifteen minutes looking at
pornographic pictures, arousing himself before he had
sex with her. This is, in reality, adultery that is committed in the mind. Mental fantasies are equally wrong.
If a man is thinking about his secretary, or another
woman somewhere else, while making love to his
wife, he's certainly not confining his affections to her.
There is no place in a Christian man's life for pornog-
raphy of any kind, be it on paper or on celluloid.
American people are spending billions on pornogra-
phy. There is a four billion dollar profit on porno-
graphy a year (see Jeremiah, David, "The Porno

Plague," *The Rebirth of America*, [Arthur DeMoss Foundation, 1986], 99). I believe close to 90 percent is purchased by men, many of whom are married.

Set your affections exclusively on your wife, and if you are having a hard time doing that, talk openly to her about it and admit your own fault. A man cannot justify in any way "looking in other pastures," be they other women or pictures of other women. Don't allow "your springs to overflow in the streets."

Respect Your Wife's Comfort Zone

Many times men are frustrated because their wives won't do to them in sex what they've heard or read other women do to and for their husbands. Usually oral sex is the real issue for the man. First, let me say that couples need to be open in communicating what is acceptable and comfortable and what isn't. No husband has the right to *demand* his wife perform oral sex on him. To do that is not walking in love. Each spouse needs to learn to ask, "Is there anything you want me to do that I'm not doing?" If something is suggested and it's repulsive to the other partner, forget it! The rule is: Is this *mutually* acceptable? Again, men need to realize that the bedroom isn't the place to exercise their "rights." The bedroom is a place to fulfill responsibilities. Oral sex between two married people who are totally faithful to each other is permissible *only* if *both* are perfectly comfortable with it. If a wife is not comfortable with oral sex, a husband, out of deference, must honor that and never insist on it.

Methods, times, places, positions, and so on, must be mutually agreed upon. Neither partner, and especially the husband, should ever "force," "insist," or "demand" anything that will take the other out of his or her sexual comfort zone. To ignore that standard means we have turned sex into lust instead of love.

Practice Tenderness

There is no place in sex for being rough, verbally or physically. Those attitudes, far from proving a man's "manliness," only confirm his perversion. The Bible says: "Husbands, love your wives and do not be *harsh* with them" (Colossians 3:19, emphasis added).

Nothing is worse than for a man to proceed with sex even when his wife has requested not to because she's not feeling well or because she's extremely tired or because her emotions are off-key for that particular time. That kind of insensitivity builds a wall that just gets thicker and thicker. Again, the adage holds true: when a man enters into the sex act for the sake of the good and pleasure of his spouse, tenderness always prevails. When he does it for personal physical gratification, the harshness comes through loud and clear.

Never, Never Criticize Your Wife's Response

The *unpardonable* word for a husband to speak to his wife is *frigid.* Nothing is more demeaning than for a husband to complain loud and long that his wife "rejected him" or "turned him off" or "set up a roadblock." Many a husband has put his wife on a horrible guilt trip in making her feel she has failed him by denying him sex when he wanted it. If your wife isn't enthusiastic about sex, maybe the best thing to do is simply hold her until you both have fallen asleep. This sends a definite message to her that you love her, even during those times she's unresponsive.

Sex is a vital part of the marriage relationship, but it's not the whole thing. It's important through it all to openly communicate with each other, with the husband taking the lead in that department.

Vexed over sex? Try tenderness, love, understanding, patience, waiting, and having a sense of fulfilling responsibility rather than getting what you want. It works every time.

5

PASTOR YOUR FLOCK!

O ne glance at the chapter title might find most of you saying, "Well, this chapter is not for me; it's for husbands who happen to be pastors of churches. My occupation happens to be_____."

Hang on men! If you don't know it yet, every husband is a "pastor." Only a fraction of them pastor local congregations. *All*, however, pastor their wives and children, if they have children. A husband's ordination to be a pastor occurred when he recited his wedding vows, and his ordination certificate is his wedding license. His flock isn't gathered in a church building, but in his house. Make no mistake about it: every husband is called by God to pastor his family. He is the high priest of his marriage and home, and needs to function that way.

We are told a great deal about Jesus' home life when we read Luke 2:52: "And Jesus grew in wisdom and stature, and in favor with God and men." How did

He grow? Did the local synagogue ruler call on Him and get Him interested in the children and teen ministry down the street? No, He grew because Joseph assumed his role as pastor and priest of his household.

Now, you and your family may belong to a church in your neighborhood. I hope you do. But your first obligation is to the church in your house. You may not have the largest congregation in town, but there is none more important. It's your performance there first that counts with God. You may be on four committees at your local church, sing in the choir, and hold three offices, but if your church at home sags because of your inadequate spiritual leadership, none of the other will matter much.

The primary source of your wife's spiritual upbuilding shouldn't come from the pastor of your local church, though he plays a part. It primarily comes from you.

"But," you're saying, "I've never been to seminary, and I'm not a Bible scholar, and I don't even have reverend in front of my name. I'm just an eight-to-five working man, and have all I can do to provide food, clothing, and shelter for my family." Well, take heart, I have good news for you. You don't have to be a Bible scholar or even be able to recite all the books of the Bible backward and forward, but there are some bottom line credentials you do need.

He who would pastor others in a spiritual way must himself be a spiritual person. That's where you start. It's impossible to pastor your wife into the things of

God if you don't know that God yourself. You begin by accepting Jesus Christ as your personal Savior and Lord.

The Bible tells us we're all sinners, that we've missed the target, the bull's eye, which is total righteousness. It further teaches us that sin separates us from God (see Isaiah 59:2). Since we cannot save ourselves (see Psalms 49:7–9), Jesus died on the cross for us, because the shedding of innocent blood was required to remove sin (see Hebrews 9:22). If we believe in Him, that He died and rose again, and are willing to confess that, we will be saved (see Romans 10:9–10). Have you received Christ as your Lord and Savior? If not, I urge you to do that right now, by inviting Him into your life through a simple prayer.

> Lord, I [your name] know that I'm a sinner, and confess that to You. Lord Jesus, I believe You died on the cross for me and rose again on the third day. Come into my heart right now, as I receive You as my Lord and my Savior. Amen.

The next thing to do after receiving Christ is find a church and be buried with your Lord in believer's baptism, which becomes the outward demonstration of the inward reality. That outward burial in water announces the inward burial and resurrection that has taken place when you believed.

Then you need to nail down the absolute *assurance* of your salvation. Jesus wanted us to be able to be sure we know we're saved so Satan won't push us around and cause us to constantly doubt. The Apostle John said, "I write these things to you who believe in the name of the Son of God so that you may know that you have eternal life" (1 John 5:13). Jesus said, "I tell you the truth, he who believes *has* everlasting life" (John 6:47, emphasis added). The fact we have eternal life is born out in the fruit we bear as well as the name we wear (see John 15:8).

No other human being can give you assurance of salvation; only the Lord can. If He says you're saved when you receive Christ, then you're saved. Don't depend on feelings and "goose bumps." God never intended that our emotions be indicators of our position in Christ. If a husband is insecure about his salvation, wavering on his position, he will not be able to lead his wife and family spiritually.

Next comes the issue of growing as a Christian. Unless you are growing, maturing, getting stronger and stronger in your effectiveness and your knowledge about Christ, you will have a tough time leading your family spiritually. You will draw them no closer to Jesus Christ than you are. They will rise no taller in their faith than your faith.

Maybe by now you're saying, "How do I know whether or not I'm growing as a Christian?" Below is a short spiritual inventory for you to take. You won't need to think long about your honest response to the statements. Circle *Yes* or *No.*

- I read from the Bible some every-   *Yes   No*
  day.

- I take a definite time to pray daily.   *Yes   No*

- I work on memorizing Scripture.   *Yes   No*

- I read at least one Christian book   *Yes   No*
  yearly.

- I ask my (fiancée) wife to pray   *Yes   No*
  with me.

- I fast for my family.   *Yes   No*

- I desire a closer relationship with   *Yes   No*
  Christ.

- I tell others about Christ.   *Yes   No*

- I enjoy worshiping and praising   *Yes   No*
  God both publicly and privately.

- I listen to Christian tapes.   *Yes   No*

No inventory is infallible, and this one is no exception. But if you're honest, I think you'll find it quite revealing. If you have more than three no answers, you may not be growing very well as a Christian husband.

Maybe you're a pragmatist, and you're saying as you read this chapter, "Come on, tell me some concrete things to do in order to pastor my family." Let me remind you first that it's the husband and father's place to initiate spiritual things in the home. When

God gave instruction to Israel concerning its children, it went without saying that this instruction was given primarily to the husband, the father of the house:

> These commandments that I give you today are to be upon your hearts. Impress them on your children. Talk about them when you sit at home and when you walk along the road, when you lie down and when you get up. Tie them as symbols on your hands and bind them on your foreheads. Write them on the doorframes of your houses and on your gates. (Deuteronomy 6:6-9)

That's a big order, and it says a lot, but it really says only one thing. Let the teaching of God's Word and God's principles pervade your house — at leisure, at work, at bedtime, and at breakfast. The question is how, in this age of everyone going in so many different directions, do we pull this off?

Talk to Your Wife about Spiritual Things

That doesn't mean a sermon every day, but even in casual conversation, weave in thoughts about God's Word and the Lord, how He's working in your life. Some men will share a testimony of how God is working in their lives with everyone else except their wives. She would love to hear about an answer to prayer. It lets her know you do pray at times other than meals.

Initiate Prayer for the Family
at Appropriate Times

I've been in so many homes for dinner where the wife is the one to say, "Well, who's going to pray?" It's almost like the husband is spiritually paralyzed and just sits there, having abrogated authority to his wife.

What are "appropriate" times? When sickness invades, prior to trips, before decisions are made, at times of great financial need, to name only a few. Let the idea of praying come from the husband; you be the initiator!

Establish the Family Altar in Your Home

I'm not necessarily talking about a piece of furniture, but rather a time either daily, weekly, or monthly when you call the whole family together. That may be only you and your wife. If you have children, it will mean them. Some Scripture is read, sharing done, praying done, and you've had a family altar. It isn't complicated; it just needs to be done at a time and a place determined by the husband.

Protect Your Family from Satan's Attacks

Satan is attacking the family today more than he's attacking any other segment of our society. He knows that as goes the family, so goes the nation. Be the official "screener" of what can be viewed on television, what books and magazines can be brought in, what movies may be rented. Take the initiative to ensure that your family has good, clean recreational fun.

Expose Your Family
to Faith-Building Events

When was the last time *you* suggested your family go to a Christian concert, a Christian seminar, or a Christian movie? In most homes those urgings usually come from the wife, not the husband. It really ought to be the other way around.

Challenge Your Family
to Scripture Memorization

If you don't, who will? Why not initiate a simple challenge for your family to learn John 15 over a one-month period? You hold them accountable, you encourage them to learn, and you learn with them. They'll remember that long after they've forgotten a lot else.

Lead Your Own Family
to Christ and Disciple Them

The best evangelist for your family is you, husband and dad. The best person to lead your children to the

Lord is you. The best person to disciple them is you. Take the initiative here, and don't abrogate that to your pastor, youth pastor, or youth sponsors.

Teach Your Family the Importance of the Tithe

I know one father and husband that makes a short ceremony out of tithing before the eyes of his family. He has them sit down while he writes out the check, has them all lay their hands on it, thank God for being able to give, and then pray for the ministries it will help. Can you imagine what kind of learning that provides for the children?

Do Something Special on Special Occasions

It may be Mother's Day, Thanksgiving, Christmas, Easter, Fourth of July, Memorial Day. Let it be a unique time for you to gather the family to pray. It's your job to pull the family together for prayer at times of illness, death, and emergencies.

As Husband and Father, You Buy and Present the Needed Bibles

There is something about receiving a Bible from one's father or husband that delivers a message. It says that in his scale of priorities, Jesus Christ is really number one, and the family follows.

Are these things impossible to pull off? Not at all. In the words of the old hymn written by William P. Merrill: "Rise up O men of God! Have done with lesser things; Give heart and soul and mind and strength to serve the King of Kings."

Pastor your flock, husbands! The rewards will be incalculable!

6

WHEN IT COMES
TO MONEY

B arry looked like a licked man. "Pastor, we're in
trouble — deep trouble." I could tell by the look
on his face, he wasn't kidding. He unfolded before me
the financial history of his thirteen years of marriage to
Andrea. They had violated every Biblical financial
principle there is. Like millions of American couples,
they had managed to live "just on the *outskirts* of their
income." Not only were they in debt up to their ears,
but he at least showed the scars of continual bickering
and fighting for thirteen years.

The issue? Money! Barry was honest; he held nothing back as he disclosed to me Andrea's unbridled and
undisciplined spending habits. In Barry's words, "We
have a cooperative plan of finances. I earn it and she
spends it."

As a top sales manager in his company, Barry had an above average income, much higher than the average man his age in business. Yet due to lack of leadership and extremely poor management, they didn't own their own home but were still renting, had zero in savings, and monthly credit card payments that almost exceeded an average house payment! At the pace they were going, they had about three months left before total disaster came, and they would lose everything but the shirts on their backs.

After a few questions, my suspicions were confirmed. As a husband, Barry, through negligence, had allowed their finances to become a shambles. Like so many husbands, he thought if he ignored it long enough and continued to be passive, the problem would go away. It only grew worse!

Two Extremes

Husbands go to two extremes when it comes to money in marriage. Check the profiles, and see if you fit either one.

Mr. Scrooge I. Control

He is the husband who basically doesn't trust anyone with his money, especially his wife. He rules with an iron fist and holds his wife accountable for how every penny is spent. He totally controls the checkbook and keeps it locked out of his wife's sight. She pays no bills, writes no checks, is allowed to see no balances, and never knows where they stand financially. She spends no money, except as he doles it out for specifics. Mr. Control gives his wife a set amount for groceries, and that's about it. It seldom is near enough and never rises with inflation. Shopping for her personal needs in the areas of new clothing, shoes, and make-up are allowed all too seldom, and then as a "bonus." His key characteristic is *control.* He must know every detail every time she asks for money. Most explanations aren't adequate for him. She is made to feel guilty for even asking for legitimate needs. This man sees nothing wrong with going out and buying new golf clubs for himself, but shrinks back in horror if his wife asks for a new washing machine because the old one keeps breaking down. This man controls his wife with money. He uses it to bribe and persuade. Few marriages survive this kind of distrust that is perpetrated in the name of "being the head of the house."

Mr. B. Passive

He is just the opposite. The closest he ever gets to money is when he endorses his paycheck, hands it to his wife, and wipes his hands clean of all financial responsibility from then on out. He places all of the burden of family finances on his wife, because he doesn't have time to do it. He is like an ostrich, sticking his head in the sand and not wanting to hear about the fact that there is too much month left over at the end of the money. His wife must decide whether to buy a service contract on the clothes dryer, how much to put in savings, how much to give the church, how much to pay the baby-sitter, and so on. He makes no financial decisions at all but relegates that to his wife. Not only is she required to carry the financial "privilege" of being the chief banker of the household, she also must bear the responsibility when there isn't enough to go around.

Mr. B. Passive gives no input, provides no direction, never discusses financial goals, and is, in general an "avoider" when it comes to money. He never looks at a bank statement and growls only when he wants to buy something, but there isn't enough money in the bank to cover it.

Positive Directions

Both extremes are obviously the wrong position for a husband to take. As the head of his marriage, he is permitted to delegate the authority of paying bills and balancing the checkbook to his efficient wife, but with loving and caring supervision. He is not free to badger, withhold funds, and use money as a lever to get what he wants. When a husband loves his wife like Christ loves the church, there will be no room for such moves.

Many marriage vows read, "till *debt* do us part." I think more marriages fail because of misuse and abuse of money on the part of the husband than for any other reason. What then are the proper directions for a husband concerning money?

Decide That Your Family Will Live Within Your Income

Our materialistic, greedy culture would say the opposite. "Whatever it takes, raise your standard of living yearly." Usually what it takes is an overextension of credit until we cannot crawl out the deep hole of debt. Many couples end up borrowing to pay off credit card bills which they ran up because they didn't have the cash or the money in the bank. It's the "buy now and pay later" generation. Consumer debt in the U.S. continues to spiral at a staggering rate. I am told that both consumer and business debt in America now exceeds six billion dollars. We know little or nothing about the delay of gratification. Husbands, don't allow your family to be ensnared by this trap, and don't raise your standard of living on the altar of debt—it's too costly a sacrifice. This takes conviction and a resolute commitment, but it's worth it.

I know this doesn't sit well, but ultimately the husband must assume the responsibility for wrecked finances in a marriage in most cases. Remember, the Bible says, "the borrower is servant to the lender" (Proverbs 22:7). Debt can destroy your marriage; don't let it.

Make Sure You Tithe Your Gross Income before You Attempt to Pay the Bills

This is where many men lose heart. They panic with, "I can't afford to tithe right now. It just won't work." Says who? God? No, says you. I don't know of any family whose finances are being blessed by God when they're not tithing.

> "Bring the whole tithe into the storehouse, that there may be food in my house. Test me in this," says the LORD Almighty, "and see if I will not throw open the floodgates of heaven and pour out so much blessing that you will not have room enough for it." (Malachi 3:10)

The husband must decide to spiritually lead the family in this holy act. He can set an example — either good or bad — that will not be forgotten by his wife and children. No amount of talking about the tithe will ever substitute for the action of tithing. Husbands and fathers, we teach by doing.

Pray with Your Wife over Major Purchases

Do you need a car? A new refrigerator? A new dryer? A second car? What about new carpet for the house? New kitchen cabinets? New outside paint job? Let your wife know you're depending on God to supply all of your needs. "And my God will meet all your needs according to his glorious riches in Christ Jesus" (Philippians 4:19). Give God the opportunity to provide the funds instead of just going to the bank to borrow. What a lesson in faith this will teach your whole family.

Ask these questions: Do we *really* need this? Do we have the money to buy it? If not, can it wait? How will God be glorified?

Force Yourself to Save

Americans have a hard time saving money. We are a consumer nation of people. Most average couples today are on a tight budget, yet the man who saves nothing from his income invites disaster in the future. Christian economists differ on how much to save. Most suggest somewhere between 5 percent and 10 percent of net income. Even if you can only save 3 percent, do it. Put it down as a fixed monthly expense and faithfully bank it where it will draw the greatest amount of interest. It may mean depriving yourselves of some luxuries as you go along, or lowering your living standard just a small amount, but it will be worth it years later.

Avoid Impulse Buying

Impulse buying occurs when you're strolling through the mall and spot something that suits your fancy, and you think, *"I've got to have that . . . especially since it's on sale this weekend."* Impulse buying is allowing the "peddlers of wares" to suggest their items to you, creating by slick marketing procedures a panting desire on your part for their product. A good rule for you to get across to your family is this: *Never go shopping without a list which also contains the maximum price you're willing to pay for the items.*

Some people shop as a hobby. They go, they look, their appetites are whetted, and they buy, not out of a sense of need, but out of a sense of "it seemed like such a good bargain." A good rule to remember is this: when tempted to buy on the spot something you didn't go to buy, make yourself wait one more day.

Live by Some Kind of a Budget

Yes, budgets do work. The best kind of a budget is to list on a sheet your fixed expenses (rent, utilities, premiums, taxes, car payments, etc.), then on another sheet your nonfixed expenses (clothing, car repair, entertainment, hobbies, gifts for others, groceries, toiletries, etc.). Determine as a couple what your normal "needs" are under nonfixed items, and set a rule not to exceed those maximums unless there is an emergency. One couple did it this way. They placed cash in paper bags every payday, drawing out funds as needed. When the cash was gone, even if it were six days before next payday, they spent no more on that item, and they made a rule not to shift funds from one bag to another. That's a bit extreme, but it does create discipline if that's what you need. All budgets need some flexibility, but as the God-ordained head of the family, husbands need to be the CEO of the finance department.

Keep No Financial Secrets

I would estimate after more than thirty years of counseling that in over half of all marriages one partner makes purchases and financial decisions without the other partner's knowledge. Make sure there is total transparency in all your financial dealings. Many men today are addicted to gambling and do not want their wives to know they're spending money "at the tracks." This is the prelude to the breakup of marriages. Have no financial secrets from each other of any kind.

Avoid the "Bigger and Better" Syndrome

That's the syndrome that says when you get a nice increase in pay or receive an inheritance, you are somehow obligated to get a nicer, bigger home, a newer, more expensive car, or take more exotic vacations. Says who? Our modern American culture, that's who. When a salary goes from thirty-three thousand dollars to forty thousand dollars most couples reason, "Wow, we've got over five hundred dollars *more* a month to spend. We can afford larger house payments, car payments, etc., so let's go for it." It seldom dawns on people to say, "Wow, over five hundred dollars more a month — that means we can increase our giving, save more for retirement, or help our aging parents more."

It is an American theme that couples *must* constantly increase their standard of living. Increasing your standard of living is not wrong in and of itself, if that's needed. But if a $120 thousand house is adequate for my family, why, if my salary increases to qualify me to get into a $175 thousand one, *must* I "move up"?

Again, because the wrong view of money has destroyed many marriages, husbands need to assume great responsibility here, as men who must give an account to God for what He has entrusted to them. Many marriages have as their vow: Till *debt* do us part. It is parting more marriages now than death. You, however, can beat those odds.

7

LEARN TO FORGIVE

I t was a six-page, handwritten, single-spaced letter, written on both sides. I could feel the pain in every line I read. The letter was from Peggy, whose twelve-year marriage to Matt had changed her into a docile, passive woman who felt inferior. She mentioned four out of scores of examples of mistakes she had made for which Matt never once forgave her. She told of living in a progressively dark, "solitary confinement" type of relationship with him. She had become paranoid about life and was afraid to even cook a meal for fear he would again find fault and be unforgiving. She had even been blamed for the birth of their third child in not taking the necessary precautions and thus getting pregnant. The once bright-eyed, cheerful, and talkative Peggy had been changed into another woman by lack of proper love and forgiveness.

Peggy, unfortunately, is not an exceptional situation. Many husbands have a critical, unforgiving spirit that has a way of changing their wives into different people.

Four Keys to Forgiveness

When couples come to me to be married, the very first question I ask both of them is, "Are you both forgiving people?" I believe this is the first prerequisite to the survival and success of any marriage. I have discovered that the culprit in the forgiveness department is usually the husband. Somehow the wife seems to have a greater capacity to forgive than the husband in the average marriage.

Husbands especially need to learn how to forgive the offenses, mistakes, judgment errors, and goofs of their wives. This can only be done by understanding what the keys of forgiveness are in the Bible. I believe there are four major keys.

1. Develop Some Blindness to the Mistakes of Your Wife

Edwin Markham, in his poem *Outwitted*, said:

> He drew a circle that shut me out
> Heretic, rebel, a thing to flout,
> But love and I had the wit to win,
> We drew a circle that took him in!

It's called the "wider circle" principle. When you've been offended, you need to draw a circle

around the one who offended you. There is no defense
to that kind of loving response. I have never known a
marriage to fall apart that practiced that principle.

You need to develop a little blindness to the sins of
others—especially your spouse. This is not to say
we're to minimize sin or rationalize mistakes away, or
that we develop a "Pollyanna" attitude that never ac-
knowledges anyone or anything is wrong. It just means
if we're loving our wives like Christ loves the church,
we'll overlook those offenses and recognize they were
done in human weakness: "Love covers over a multi-
tude of sins" (1 Peter 4:8).

We are prone to take everything extremely personally; thus it's hard for most to overlook an offense. Yet
the Scripture says: "It is to his glory to overlook an
offense" (Proverbs 19:11).

Some husbands find themselves saying harsh things
when their wives have made a mistake. "Oh, you did it
again, huh?" or "Boy, you've done it this time," or "Is
your middle name, Mistake?" How much better to take
your wife in your arms, hold her closely, and say,
"That's all right, honey. I've done things much worse
than that. Don't give it another thought."

2. When You Have Trouble Forgiving, Remember Your Own Sins

Before you withhold forgiveness from your wife, just
remember that you have sinned too. You have made
mistakes, maybe not the same kind, but just as serious.

In the words of Solomon: "Who can say, 'I have kept my heart pure; I am clean and without sin'?" (Proverbs 20:9).

The Bible is full of warnings about remembering our own proneness to sin, our own weakness and tendency to live beneath the highest and best we know. "Brothers, if someone is caught in a sin, you who are spiritual should restore him gently. *But watch yourself, or you also may be tempted*" (Galatians 6:1, emphasis added).

I have found that when I have trouble forgiving my spouse, one quick look at my sins tells me I'm not qualified to withhold forgiveness. "Be kind and compassionate to one another, forgiving each other, just as in Christ God forgave you" (Ephesians 4:32). Well, if we're to forgive others as God in Christ forgave us, the question is, how did God in Christ forgive us?

He forgave us unconditionally and freely. There was not one sin He didn't cover. He didn't say, "Well, I'll forgive this, but not this. I'll pardon 35 percent of this, but not this." He freely forgave us, and unless we think we're greater than God, we need to freely forgive others, especially our spouse.

3. Don't Seek to Even the Score

There is something in all of us that wants to "get 'em back." In marriage there is no place for revenge, no place to "pay back." Even Solomon learned that: "Do not say, 'I'll pay you back for this wrong!' Wait for the Lord, and he will deliver you" (Proverbs 20:22).

You may think you're getting revenge, but you really aren't. What you're really doing is confusing the whole thing and interfering with God's process in the offender's life. That's why Paul said:

> Do not repay anyone evil for evil. Be careful to do what is right in the eyes of everybody. If it is possible, as far as it depends on you, live at peace with everyone. Do not take revenge, my friends, but leave room for God's wrath, for it is written, "It is mine to avenge; I will repay," says the Lord. (Romans 12:17-19)

Revenge is one responsibility God never intended any man to assume. That belongs in His department, and He will do a complete, thorough job because He is all-knowing. You will only do a partial job. When it comes to getting even, why not let the One do it who alone will do it right?

When the Pharisees brought the woman caught in the act of adultery to Jesus saying that she should be stoned, they got an answer they weren't expecting. Jesus said, "If any one of you is without sin, let him be the first to throw a stone at her" (John 8:7). Beginning with the older ones, they began to go away one by one. Jesus and the woman stood alone facing each other. He asked her where her accusers were, and who was left to condemn her? Then He said, "Then neither do I condemn you. . . . Go now and leave your life of

sin" (John 8:11). Notice this: Jesus didn't justify her
sin; He forgave it. He didn't say her mistake wasn't
sin; He simply emphasized the fact that He didn't
come to condemn, but to save. That's the spirit with
which we need to be forgiving our wives.

4. Let There Be an Attitude of Softness, Not Rigidity

This last key to forgiveness is important because simply saying "I forgive you" doesn't make it so. It's how
we say it, the tone of voice, the attitude that counts.
The Bible tells us that we're to submit to one another
(see Ephesians 5:21). This means there is to be a sense
of humility in our hearts as we extend our love and
forgiveness to others. Scripture also teaches that our
speech is to be seasoned with salt, full of grace, and
that kindness is to be in the tone of our voice (see
Colossians 4:6).

To withhold forgiveness from your spouse, letting
her sweat it out, is not only ungodly, but it is also at-
tempting to elevate yourself higher than God. It is a
presumptuous thing we have no right to do as a husband. Perhaps Paul summed it up best when he wrote:

> Therefore, as God's chosen people, holy and dearly
> loved, clothe yourselves with compassion, kindness,
> humility, gentleness and patience. Bear with each
> other and *forgive* whatever grievances you may
> have against one another. Forgive as the Lord for-
> gave you. And over all these virtues put on love,

which binds them all together in perfect unity. (Colossians 3:12–14, emphasis added)

Keep the Slate Clean

Companies that manufacture pencils put erasers on the other end. They know from experience that those who use pencils are human and make mistakes. We need to live in our marriages with erasers ready. We'll need them, and our spouse will need them for us as well.

A marriage and family counselor in my community confided in me recently that he has seen again and again couples come to him with deep-seated bitterness, holding tightly on to grudges and animosities that literally change them into someone they really don't like. He has seen them become physically ill to the point of hospitalization because of nursed grudges they refuse to release.

Husbands desperately need to initiate the healing of hurts, offenses, and wrongs, even when they're not in the wrong. It comes with the turf of headship, men. Don't wait for your wife to come crawling to you to say, "I'm sorry." You have the responsibility by virtue of your office as husband to initiate reconciliation.

Delay or refusal to forgive quickly brings scars into a relationship that won't heal overnight. The best method is simply forgive swiftly. Marriages built on "keeping score" usually crumble. This list of "nevers" will protect you from the pitfalls of unforgiveness. Remember that the responsibility and authority for reconciliation are yours.

- *Never* say, "I forgive you, but you must live with the consequences."

- *Never* bring up past offenses of your spouse as a "lever" to get something you want.

- *Never* use your forgiveness to get something you want.

- *Never* allow the sun to go down without extending pardon.

- *Never* give partial forgiveness.

- *Never* "negotiate" forgiveness or make it conditional.

Keep the slate clean, and determine that Satan will not get a foothold in your marriage in this area especially.

I've never known a husband who regretted forgiving his wife, even when the offense was deep. I've had plenty of men, however, tell me they wish they could do it all over again, and this time they would freely forgive and extend their affection.

There is one marriage Satan cannot spoil: It's the marriage whose blackboard of offenses is erased daily. Grab those erasers, men and erase like crazy!

8

BE A FITNESS BUFF

F itness is in today. Men and women are working out, jogging, swimming, and hiking to keep the biceps round and the tummy flat. It's hopefully more than just a fad. Keeping fit keeps heart attacks down and energy up.

But there's another kind of fitness that's even more vital than physical fitness. "For physical training is of some value, but godliness has value for all things, holding promise for both the present life and the life to come" (1 Timothy 4:8). In other words, physical fitness helps us in this life only, while spiritual fitness benefits us in this life and the next.

If someone invented a survival kit for husbands to get them through the lifelong challenge of "husbandhood," I know one item that would be absolutely necessary: an instruction sheet on how to have a successful D.Q.T. What is a "D.Q.T."? It is what I call a *D*aily *Q*uiet *T*ime, a time alone with God apart from the noise, the rush, and the *busy*ness of the daily grind of work and other obligations. It will become the most important time of your day, a time when the gut-level issues of life are thought through, prayed through, and settled. Most Christian men neglect this to their peril. They survive for awhile, but sooner or later they are driven to the prayer closet.

Steps to Spiritual Fitness

We've already talked about the importance of being a high priest to your wife, being the spiritual leader of your home, the initiator of spiritual things in your marriage. We've talked about the importance of discussing the Bible and praying with your wife. But none of those things can substitute for developing your own spiritual life and deepening your own relationship with God. That can only come about by clearing a time and a place to have a daily quiet time.

If you are really serious about wanting to strengthen your spiritual life, read on. Here are the steps, and it's important that you take them sequentially and thoroughly.

1. Determine the Need

Before you do anything, determine that a daily quiet time is not optional in your life, as a man of God and as a husband. Decide now that it's nonnegotiable and not up for vote. It's a *must*.

I was a few years into my ministry before I put this on the front burner in my life. I would pray occasionally, read my Bible when preparing a message, but I had not established a disciplined time in my life to be alone with no one but God. Then one day I heard a devotional by a layman at a prayer breakfast. He used only one Scripture reference, but it was enough to convict me. "Very early in the morning, while it was still dark, Jesus got up, left the house and went off to a solitary place, where he prayed" (Mark 1:35).

It didn't take me long to reason this: If Jesus, the divine Son of God, the incarnate Deity, sinless in every way, sensed the need to get alone with God on a regular basis, who did I think I was that I could survive spiritually without the same practice?

I also determined something else. Jesus said: "I no longer call you servants, because a servant does not know his master's business. Instead, I have called you *friends*, for everything that I learned from my Father I have made known to you" (John 15:15, emphasis added). Jesus is not only my Savior, but my friend. Friends love to get together and fellowship and talk. I suddenly realized that if I'm Jesus' friend — and I am — He desires companionship with me, and I ought to desire companionship with Him. I realize we can experience that companionship throughout the day, but there needs to be a special time when we're alone together for intimate conversation and fellowship. That time is my daily quiet time. It's the nature of friends to get together and talk. So from God's perspective, a daily quiet time is quite natural, though to man, in his weakness, it may seem unnatural and unnecessary. We need to get to know our Savior better and better.

So before you do anything, decide in your heart how necessary a daily quiet time is for you.

2. Determine the Time

I haven't met many men lately who tell me they have time on their hands. I used to think a great big block of time would just drop out of the sky for me to be alone with God. I discovered that I had to *clear* the time, or a daily quiet time would remain a wish, never a reality.

No one should get legalistic about a time. Some have their daily quiet time in the evenings before bedtime. Others have had success doing it over the lunch hour, while others have been most successful in the mornings. For men, I strongly suggest the mornings for the following reasons.

First of all, it was the time Jesus chose. Remember, Mark's account says, "very early in the morning, while it was still dark" (1:35). In essence He did it before the day got under way. It was such a priority in His life that He simply got up earlier to experience God's presence before the onslaught of the daily schedule. Secondly, I believe our mind is clearest shortly after we awake from a night's rest. Our attention hasn't been worn down yet with disputes, tensions, pressures, and decisions. Personally I found it next to impossible to concentrate in the evenings with the weight of a whole day of seeing and talking with people on my mind. I would be giving God the leftovers of my attention. Thirdly, in the morning we should put on the whole armor of God for the battles of the day. We need to hear from God before we hear from the world. We need to read His Word before we read the morning newspaper. Psychologists tell us that we remember the longest what is put through our thought processes earliest in the day. If that's true, the case for the morning being the time for daily quiet times is very good.

Maybe you're protesting, saying, "But I already have to get up early just to get to work." Then train yourself to get up thirty minutes earlier. Of course this may also mean you need to go to bed thirty minutes earlier. Maybe you will need to sacrifice the evening news on television and go to bed. You'll find you're going to bed with positive thoughts instead of the negative ones of the news. The important thing is to set a time and keep it, letting nothing interfere with it, seeing it as much a necessity as showering, eating breakfast, or dressing.

3. Determine the Place

This may sound elementary, but I've found that every man needs to seek out a place to be alone with God. Mark tells us that Jesus went to a solitary place. It really doesn't matter where you go as long as it too is a solitary place. It must be away from phones, doorbells, television sets, radios, and other people. It may mean finding a walk-in closet, going in, and shutting the door. It may mean going out in the middle of your backyard or shutting yourself in your bathroom. I know one man who ended up going into his attic when the weather permitted just to escape the noise of his five children.

I have found it helpful in the spring and summer months to go outside on my deck or into my backyard, where I can be near the natural things God has created. In the winter, I shut myself up in my living room and draw the drapes to have the feeling of being alone with God. That way if I want to fall prostrate, stand with uplifted hands, kneel, or just sit, I'm in privacy. Wherever you go, make sure it's a solitary place where you can be alone with the Lord.

4. Determine a Definite Plan in Your Daily Quiet Time

No plan is divinely inspired. Everyone has his own agenda. I share mine, not so that it will be copied in every detail, but so you may see the possible steps to making a daily quiet time meaningful.

Practice the presence of God. Take one or two minutes before reading any Scripture, and affirm God's presence, claim it, confess it, by saying, "Lord, I know You're here, let me sense Your nearness and Your presence as I read Your Word."

Read a couple of chapters from the Old Testament.
A good starting place is the Psalms. Read them slowly,
and meditate on them as you read. You might want to
read the chapter from Proverbs whose number corre-
sponds with the day of the month. For example, on the
first day of the month read chapter one; second day,
chapter two; and so on. Proverbs has thirty-one chapters, so it works out just right.

*Read one chapter from the New Testament every
day for one month.* I've found it extremely beneficial to
read repeatedly the same chapter from a "growth section" in the New Testament. What is a growth section?
Of course all of the New Testament will help us grow,
but there are some chapters that will especially encourage and challenge us in our relationship with the Lord.
Some of those chapters are: Matthew 5, 6, 7; Luke 6;
John 6, 10, 15; Romans 12; 1 Corinthians 15; 2 Corinthians 4, 5, 8, 10; Galatians 5, 6; Ephesians 4, 5, 6;
Philippians 2; Colossians 3; 1 Thessalonians 4; 1 Peter
5; 2 Peter 3; Hebrews 11, 12, 13; all of 1 John. Why the
same chapter every day for a month? In order to let that
Word sink into your life and become a part of you.

It's usually helpful to try to memorize that New
Testament chapter after you read it each day. Try to
memorize a verse or two daily and review often.

Spend the rest of the time in prayer. Everyone has
a pattern of prayer that is especially meaningful to
them. I've found the following helpful.

- Adoration and praise

- Thanksgiving

- Confession

- Intercession and petition

- Claiming and agreeing in faith

Spend the first several minutes praising God. Sing a song to the Lord, one you know or one you create. Even if you're not a good singer, sing to the Lord. A joyful noise pleases God as much as quality sound. Spend some time praising God for who He is. He is:

- Jehovah-jireh, your provider

- Jehovah-nissi, your banner

- Jehovah-shalom, your peace

- Jehovah-rophi, your healer

- Jehovah-shammah, the God who is there

- Jehovah-rohi, your shepherd

- Jehovah-tsidkinu, your righteousness.

Then spend some time thanking Him for His blessings. Confess your sin to Him in accordance with 1 John 1:9: "If we confess our sins, he is faithful and just and will forgive us our sins and purify us from all unrighteousness." Affirm His forgiveness as He promised. Next, intercede for others, using a prayer list. This includes your spouse, your children, parents, siblings, your boss, people you would like to see saved, the sick, etc.

Finally spend a few seconds claiming and affirming God's answer.

How long does all this take? If you can afford an hour, that's great. If you want to start with fifteen minutes, then that's a start, but it would be better if you could stretch it to thirty minutes. The length of time is not nearly as important as the fact that you keep that time alone with God on a daily basis.

You will never be the husband God has called you to be until you deepen your life in a daily quiet time. Please don't see it just as something helpful, but as an essential rendezvous. You will think of a thousand excuses to miss this time with God. You'll even find yourself rationalizing to yourself and others just why you can't do that every day. Don't give in; make it a discipline in your life you're willing to live and die for. God will honor that, and your decisions about your family, your job, or anything else in your life will come much easier. Guard that time with your life.

Remember, you have a great responsibility as a husband, a superhuman task. You cannot pull that task off without quality time alone with the Lord. Nothing is more vital than developing your spiritual muscles.

Mental Fitness

Men, by nature, are task-oriented. Most men find it hard to come before the God who says, "Be still, and know that I am God" (Psalms 46:10). Unless they are writing something, building something, moving something, or changing something, they don't believe they are getting anywhere. Daily quiet times don't come easy for men, not even for pastors. It has to be cultivated, developed, and groomed before it becomes a natural part of the day.

The repeated renewing of the mind will take you from babyhood, into adolescence, and on to adulthood spiritually. But how is the mind renewed? Wouldn't it be wonderful to nightly remove your mind, soak it in bleach, then put it back in the next day? There's something even better than that. It's allowing God's Word to renew your mind.

> Be transformed by the renewing of your mind. (Romans 12:2)

> Be made new in the attitude of your minds. (Ephesians 4:23)

> Put on the new self, which is being renewed in knowledge in the image of its Creator. (Colossians 3:10)

The amount of sin we commit is directly related to the amount of God's Word we allow to imprint itself on our minds and hearts. That's why the psalmist said, "I have hidden your word in my heart that I might not sin against you" (119:11). The psalmist knew there was a direct correlation to personal purity and holiness and the Word of God: "How can a young man keep his way pure? By living according to your *word*" (Psalms 119:9, emphasis added). It's no wonder then that Paul exhorted us: "Let the word of Christ dwell in you richly as you teach and admonish one another with all wisdom" (Colossians 3:16). Since the mind gets soiled daily, it needs renewal and cleansing daily, and only as we're into God's Word, even if it's only a few short verses, will that effective cleansing come.

Because I'm a pragmatist and know the proneness of men, here's a simple formula to get you started in a daily quiet time, beginning *tomorrow:* Read John 15 daily for the next seven days, and commit yourself to pray right after you read.

The next time someone else who read this book says to you, "How's your D.Q.T.?" you can honestly say, "I'm on my way."

9

DISCIPLINE
YOUR CHILDREN

A nn forced out the words. Ashamed to let me
know what her home life was really like, she
hedged until I finally said, "What's the real issue,
Ann?" In tears she divulged what to me had become a
familiar story about an absent husband and father. Dale
traveled two to three days a week. Job pressure and his
own temperament made him the absent father, even
when he was home. The heaviest burden to her was the
fact that 100 percent of the discipline of their four children was left entirely to her, whether Dale was home
or not. His only comment to her was that he was too
tired to be bothered with it. She was at the end of her
rope as the children were reaching the age where they
were seriously challenging her authority. Dale neither
backed her up nor disputed her word with the kids; it
was as though he were not even there.

There are many Dales; you may be one reading this now. As the God-ordained director of your home, the husband of your wife, and father of your children, you are called to be the CEO of discipline in your home. No, this doesn't mean the husband is to do all the discipline, but he is to be interested, active, vitally involved, and supportive of his wife, especially when he is unable to be physically present.

The writer of Hebrews speaks of the naturalness of fathers disciplining their children when he writes:

> Endure hardship as discipline; God is treating you as sons. For what son is not disciplined by his father? If you are not disciplined (and everyone undergoes discipline), then you are illegitimate children and not true sons. Moreover, we have all had human fathers who disciplined us and we respected them for it. (Hebrews 12:7-9)

God's Purpose in Discipline

According to 1 Samuel 3 God brought judgment against Eli because he knew that his sons had made themselves contemptible, yet he did nothing about it. He failed to exercise any kind of discipline to restrain them. Not only were his sons put to death, but God also said that Eli's sin would never be atoned for (1 Samuel 3:14). That's a harsh judgment, but I think it underscores how seriously God takes the husband and father being involved in discipline.

Discipline is certainly not pleasant, but it is necessary. And, men, we need to seriously consider God's purpose for requiring it in the home.

To Weave Judgment into Our Children

Proverbs tells us, "Wisdom is found on the lips of the discerning, but a rod is for the back of him who lacks judgment" (10:13). The strong provision of guidelines and parameters a father provides for his child is God's way of bringing a sense of right judgment into the child's life.

To Adequately Prepare Your Child for the Future

"Train a child in the way he should go, and when he is old he will not turn from it" (Proverbs 22:6). That's a famous verse that has often been misunderstood.

It's important to remember that it reads, "the way *he* should go." That means discipline must be personalized. Secondly, it says when he is *old* he won't turn from it. He probably will, however, before he becomes old. Be that as it may, a father's discipline of his child is God's way for Dad to prepare him for the hard knocks the future will bring. Passivity toward discipline, or total neglect of it, means a father is deliberately guaranteeing his child won't be ready for the future.

To Rid Your Child of Folly

The Bible teaches we're all born in sin. Our depraved nature, until it is changed by the power of Jesus Christ at conversion, is full of folly, especially as a child. Solomon wisely wrote: "Folly is bound up in the heart of a child, but the rod of discipline will drive it far from him" (Proverbs 22:15). Remember, the "rod" is not the agent of a dad's anger, but the shaping tool of God's renovation.

Folly and foolishness in a five-year-old is one thing, but left unchecked and undisciplined, it often results in permanent damage to the person's life. Only the loving, yet firm discipline of a concerned father will rid that child of folly.

To Salvage a Child's Soul from Death

We're not talking about physical death here. No man can stave off physical death; it comes to all. But we are concerned with the soul of the child because that has to do with eternity. "Do not withhold discipline from a child; if you punish him with the rod, he will not die. Punish him with the rod and save his soul from death" (Proverbs 23:13–14).

Eli lost his sons' souls and bodies in death because he saw the need for discipline, yet he refused to do anything about it.

To Make Your Child a Giver of Peace and Delight

One of the great promises given to parents is found again in the book of Proverbs: "Discipline your son, and he will give you peace; he will bring delight to your soul" (29:17).

Oftentimes the lack of respect that parents see in teens is a direct result of the father failing to discipline when that teen was a small child.

To Impart Wisdom

"The rod of correction imparts wisdom" (Proverbs 29:15). No, this doesn't mean that every time you spank your children, or verbally correct them that they get smarter. But yes, it does mean that over the long haul of raising your children, consistent discipline instills a wisdom that cannot be received from a school classroom, a book, or any other way. I remember the day my father saw me mowing the yard barefoot. He quietly came over, turned the mower off, and swatted me sternly on the backside. He looked me in the eye and said, "Don't ever mow the yard without shoes. It's a quick way to lose two feet." Guess what, I never mowed the lawn again, not even once, to this day without shoes. I don't know, but I can safely guess that I have two feet on which to stand and walk today because of the temporary pain and chagrin of a swatting when I was only twelve.

Tips when Disciplining your Child

Remember, Dad, that the discipline you administer, whether with or without a rod, is not for your
temporary relief; it's not to vent your anger. Its ob-
jective is for the benefit of your child. As the Lord
disciplines those whom He loves, so we discipline
our children because we love them, not because we're
angry with them.

Here are a few simple tips to remember when disciplining your child.

- Never administer discipline because you're getting
  pressure from others like family, neighbors, or
  friends. Make sure that before you discipline, it's because you have checked out the situation thoroughly
  and are convinced that your child needs to be cor-
  rected.

- Never discipline when you're extremely angry. Cool
  off first, or your discipline will be done to make you
  feel better rather than for the benefit of your child.

- Never openly call into question your spouse's discipline of your children. This only creates confusion in
  the children. If you feel it's unjustified, talk to your
  mate in private.

- Never fail to explain to your child the reason for the
  spanking or the punishment. It's not acceptable, when
  the child asks why he is getting spanked, for the father to simply say, "Because I'm the parent and
  you're the child, and that's the way it is."

Fathers have a dual responsibility in disciplining their children: "Fathers, do not exasperate your children; instead, bring them up in the training and instruction of the Lord" (Ephesians 6:4). The word *exasperate* is translated *provoke* in some versions. The word literally means to frustrate and bring added agitation. This most commonly occurs when a child is spanked by a parent without any explanation.

Note the second part of that admonition: "Bring them up in the training and instruction of the Lord." If you notice, that command is given to the fathers, not the mothers. That doesn't mean the mother shouldn't share in the responsibility of teaching, instructing, and training (in all too many cases, she carries the responsibility alone), but it does mean that the primary responsibility of disciplining and teaching children the Word of God belongs to the *father.*

Fathers are exhorted again by Paul to " not *embitter* your children, or they will become discouraged" (Colossians 3:21, emphasis added). In the context of discipline, dads, this means that you're not to ride your child's case until you break his spirit.

There is a fine line dads need to first find, then refuse to cross, because once you've crossed that line and embittered your child, you may not be able to remedy the situation.

Clearly the father is to have a vital part in disciplining the children, not leaving all of that to the mother. God never intended that she bear the burden and responsibility of all the discipline. As a dad, that responsibility belongs primarily to you. You may delegate some of it, you may invite your wife to help you share it, but to leave it all to her is to impose a weight on her shoulders God never intended her to bear.

Priority Time not "Quality" Time

American homes are suffering today as never before from the "absent father syndrome." The pressures of job, increased social involvements, accelerated travel, plus the idea that it is in "vogue" for the dad to be gone a great deal, have all wreaked havoc on children.

I just recently read where the average father today spends an average of thirty-seven seconds daily in meaningful conversation with his children with less than three meaningful encounters per week. Stack this against the fact that the same child watches television between thirty-five and fifty-five hours per week, and you don't have to wonder who is shaping our children's values for the future (see Jeremiah, David, *Before It's Too Late* [Nashville: Thomas Nelson, Pubs., 1982], 26).

Prison chaplains tell me that a clear majority of young men incarcerated for violent crimes come from homes where a single mom raised them or from homes where their fathers were gone the majority of the time. That doesn't mean if you're gone from home an inordinate amount of time that your child will end up in prison, but it does mean that the likelihood of aberrant behavior later in life increases significantly.

The term "quality" time has been overused by busy dads to mean "I may not be able to spend a large amount of time with my child, but I make sure the little time I spend is *quality* time." I've found that children don't know the difference between quality and quantity time — except that one period is much shorter than the other. Children are not impressed with "quality" time. When they are grown, they won't much care how many awards you got at work, or how much money you made, or how many times your picture appeared in the company magazine. They will be impressed, however, with remembering that you were home, you played with them, laughed with them, worked with them, prayed with them, and listened to them. Unfortunately, one of the first questions twentieth-century American children learn to ask their moms is, "When will Daddy be home?" Many ask it again and again.

So, the bottom line is this. Fathers are to be the CEO of the discipline department of their homes. To do that, you must be home. To be home, you must clear the time and see it as a priority. Guess what? It's worth the effort.

10

THE HUSBAND BEATITUDES

When He began the Sermon on the Mount, Jesus gave nine beatitudes. These have often been called "beautiful attitudes." They are principles dealing with how to develop the kind of attitudes in our lives that will enable us to live victoriously.

Without trying to be irreverent, here are some modern "beatitudes" every husband needs to develop toward his wife.

Blessed Is He
Who Listens to His Wife

One of the most common complaints counselors hear from wives is that their husbands don't listen. They hear the noise of speech, but they don't *listen*. Men need desperately to develop listening skills. Some husbands have learned how to tune out their wife's voice, though they listen very carefully to their secretary, their boss, their mother, or even their children. Marriage doesn't automatically make a man deaf. Listen!

Blessed Is He
Who Spends Quantity and Quality Time
with His Wife

No one denies that most men are busy "up to their gills" with pressure from work, pressure from parents, in-laws, and the list goes on. Their first responsibility, however, is to their wives. Most men react, "But a guy has to make a living." More importantly, a guy has to make a marriage too, if he chooses that route. Your wife is your first time commitment apart from your job. She demands equal or more time than your hobby or your social life. Time won't drop out of the sky for you to spend with her; you have to clear the time.

Blessed Is He
Who Trusts His Wife in All Things

Every godly marriage is built on trust. Nothing devastates a wife more than to live with a husband who doesn't trust her. Sometimes the lack of trust is in her shopping, her tastes, her judgments with the kids, and how she handles money in general. It's hard for some men to let go and realize that she is bone of his bone, and flesh of his flesh. Husband, trust your wife.

Blessed Is He
Who Is Patient When His Wife Is Sick

Sooner or later your wife will be ill. It may be a migraine headache, premenstrual syndrome, asthma, arthritis, the flu, or just a common head cold. Normal, routine things won't get done. The meals won't be cooked, beds won't be made, dishes won't be washed, the carpet won't be vacuumed. Remember your wedding vows: "in *sickness* and in health." And sometimes there can be more sickness than health. Patience in sickness will make a real difference in your marriage. Remember, the day will come when you too are sick.

Blessed Is He
Who Brings Encouragement to His Wife

A husband who is a real tower of strength to his wife will bring encouragement to her. It may come in the form of complimenting her cooking, affirming her sewing, commenting on her creativity as an interior decorator, or simply making an investment in a hobby or sideline she does well. Blessed indeed is the husband who knows his wife needs to be lifted from time to time. If you, her lover, don't bring words of encouragement to her, who will?

Blessed Is He
Who Takes an Interest
in His Wife's World

A good wife's world will revolve around her husband and family, but be that as it may, she still has another world with her own interests, hobbies, and habits. Is it ceramics, cross-stitching, painting? Show her you're interested by inquiring, listening, and maybe occasionally buying a gift in the area of her interest. She needs to know that her interests matter to you as well as her.

Blessed Is He
Who Initiates Reconciliation
with His Wife

The best of marriages have differences, and sometimes they turn into cross words. Do your best to keep it from going that far, but if it does, you as the husband need to initiate reconciliation. Don't wait for her to come to you. Husbands need to learn to humble themselves before their wives. If every husband would see himself as a committee of one in his marriage to make it his business to begin the words of reconciliation, it would bring a freshness to that relationship. The Bible makes it clear: "Do not let the sun go down while you are still angry" (Ephesians 4:26).

There is no place this is more important than in marriage.

Blessed Is He
Who Does Not Abuse Headship

We've already talked about headship. The husband is the head of the wife as Christ is the head of the church (see Ephesians 5:23). God's "chain of command" doesn't mean the wife is in chains and the husband is in command! It does mean that in the institution of marriage, God has ordained the husband to be in the position of headship. It doesn't mean a man becomes the "gang-boss" of his wife. It's not "I'm the head and you must do as I say," but "God has ordained me to be the head of this union. How can I serve you or help you?"

Blessed Is He
Who Prays Daily for His Wife

I have found that one of the best ways I can stay close to my wife is to daily lift her and her needs to God in prayer. When the Bible says we're to pray for one another, that includes our spouse, first and foremost.

Maybe you're saying, "For what do I pray?" For starters, pray that God will give her a clearer understanding of *you*. If you're like most husbands, you're not easy to figure out or understand. Pray for her health, for an increase in her hunger for spiritual things, for her stamina in raising the children and being a homemaker. Pray a "hedge of thorns" around her purity and godliness that Satan will never get a foothold in allowing her to ever be interested in anyone else besides you. Pray for God to show you ways to invest in her life, so that the two of you will grow closer and closer in your commitment to each other.

Blessed Is He Who Avoids Harsh Words with His Wife

There are millions of wives today who don't have a mark on their bodies from physical abuse from their husbands, but their spirits are bleeding and bruised severely. We used to sing: "Sticks and stones may break my bones, but words will never hurt me." How untrue! You and I both know that one of the deadliest assault weapons known to man today is harsh, critical, and condemning words.

Solomon's advice is good: "Do not be quick with your mouth, do not be hasty in your heart to utter anything before God. . . . let your words be few" (Ecclesiastes 5:2).

Husbands really need to set a sentinel at the entrance of their mouth.

He who guards his lips guards his soul, but he who speaks rashly will come to ruin. (Proverbs 13:3)

As a north wind brings rain, so a sly tongue brings angry looks. (Proverbs 25:23)

Some of you are saying, "Oh, but you don't know my wife! Her tongue is sharper than my razor. Am I to be verbally assaulted, but yet I don't have the right to speak back?" Listen to what the Bible says: "A man's wisdom gives him patience; it is to his glory to over-look an offense" (Proverbs 19:11). And it's still true that "A gentle answer turns away wrath, but a harsh word stirs up anger" (Proverbs 15:1).

The poet was right:

> How like an arrow is a word
> At random often speeding
> To find a target never meant
> To set some heart a-bleeding.
> Oh, pray that Heaven may seal the lips
> E're unkind words are spoken;
> For Heaven itself cannot recall,
> When once that seal is broken.
>
> (Author Unknown)

It's no wonder Jesus said, "But I tell you that men will have to give account on the day of judgment for every careless *word* they have spoken. For by your *words* you will be acquitted, and by your *words* you will be condemned" (Matthew 12:36–37, emphasis added).

Men, you can actually set your wife's mood by your words. Paul wrote to the Colossian husbands: "Husbands, love your wives and do not be *harsh* with them" (3:19, emphasis added). It's not just the words we speak, but the tone of voice with which we speak them.

Communication is the real key, and God doesn't want you monitoring her words to you—just watch your words to her.

Blessed Is He
Who Keeps His Wife Informed

The success of a marriage, to a large degree, is commensurate with the low amount of surprises. This is why good communication is a necessity. I have found it helpful to make sure my wife's calendar by her phone reads the same as my calendar on my desk, especially in those areas where both of us are affected. This includes dinner appointments, out-of-town speaking engagements, special events, and doctor appointments.

Make sure you inform your wife of major purchases to the point of asking her opinion about them. One lady once told me she didn't know till the truck pulled up that they were having their garage remodeled into another bedroom! Obviously these little surprises can be a source of much irritation and argument.

Keep your wife informed about your health, your insurance, your estate, your plans for the future, your job, your IRA, your health club dues, your worries and cares.

One of the major complaints women have about their husbands is that they feel they're married to a total stranger. Because he never tells them what's going on, they feel left out, shut out, and put out. Keep your wife informed.

Blessed Is He
Who Does Not Always Have to Be Right

A common tendency of most husbands is that their way of doing things is the right way, and they're waiting for their wives to "get with the program." It may be anything: painting the den, mowing the lawn, washing the dishes, doing the laundry, cleaning the carpet, washing the car, making the bed, or opening the mail. The classic example is squeezing the toothpaste tube — wives squeeze in the middle and husbands squeeze at the end, which of course is the right way!

Be careful, men! As you can break the spirit of your child, you can break the spirit of your wife by insisting that she do everything your way or not at all.

One of the greatest things I learned after I was married a few years was that my way isn't necessarily the best way, the most efficient way, or even the most economical way; it's just the way I learned from growing up. It was wrong for me to foist that on my wife.

Do these beatitudes sound impossible to carry out? They are if you try alone. Only as you rely on the Lord can it be done.

ea.   ea.   ea.

Marriage is a voyage; all the sea isn't smooth. But you're in the same boat, and the key is that you sail the trip together, not against each other. And because God has appointed and ordained the husband to be the captain of the ship, the responsibility rests squarely on your shoulders for your cargo, namely your wife.

Happy sailing, mate!

11

BE A BOREDOM BUSTER

D oes your husband have a den?" the lady asked her friend. "No, he growls all over the house." Sounds like a marriage that has gone stale due to boredom. Like silent termites that eat the foundation from under a house, boredom eats silently away at a marriage, slowly, subtly, quietly, and usually unnoticed until couples wake up and say to themselves, "How boring!"

Robert was in his mid-sixties. Before I met with him, I had been told the facts by his wife. For almost a year, he had left her, come back, then left again. The attraction was a woman almost twenty years younger. I was the last person he wanted to talk to, but his wife and grown children had applied pressure and insisted, and he really had no choice. Robert owned up to everything, and then came my inevitable question:

"Why?" Why throw a marriage of forty-two years away at this time? At this age? At this juncture in his life? Ready to retire and enjoy a good retirement income so he and his wife could travel and take it easy, Robert was starting a new romance at this age. Why? In his words (they were few) he was bored with his wife, his house, his car, his job, but mostly with his wife and marriage. He put it this way: "I come home; the table is set the same way; I sit in the same place; we talk about the same things. She wears the same hairdo, the same fragrance, the same style dresses. We eat the same kinds of food, then after dinner she's glued to the tube, and I to the paper. I eventually get up, go to bed, and start another day the next morning of doing the same thing again. I want to share my life before I die with someone who is exciting, vibrant, and wants to do something different!"

Of course, what Robert couldn't see was that all of this boredom in his marriage was partly his fault. When it all came out, his wife concurred that she too was bored with him and his boredom, but due to a lack of good, clear communication, they let it go too far.

I found out one thing, when you're bored, you'll try anything; some will even try being a lover to someone twenty years younger than they are! Fortunately, this case has a happy ending. Robert is now back with his wife, they're communicating about it all, and his wanderlust has run its course. Forgiveness has been extended, and he realizes that much of his boredom was his own fault, and he has taken steps to correct it.

Are you fun to live with? Is your wife *excited* that you're home, because you don't do the same thing the same way twice? Can she honestly say that you are the "spice of life"?

Don't mistranslate what you're reading. No one is telling you that you have to become clever doing a new act every evening to keep things crisp in your marriage. You don't have to learn to do cartwheels, magic tricks, or ride a unicycle to keep the zing in your marriage. You do have to be aware that boredom and monotony can set into a marriage slowly, and a couple can lose interest in each other, quickly finding others more fun to be with. The biggest culprit is lack of awareness.

There are some definite things you can do to be a "boredom buster" in your marriage.

Don't Take Your Wife for Granted

Years ago, a man shared a short note with me that read like this:

> I'm gone. I'm not sure you'll even notice. Our lives have lost the sparkle. I'm tired of being taken for granted. Don't try to get me to come back. I've left in order to restore some interest in my life again.
> Your Wife

This man was devastated and in a state of utter shock. His words to me were, "I just thought she would always be there." That was his problem. He had come to take his wife for granted. She was "old hat" to him. He never appeared excited to see her; he just assumed she would be there with a hot meal, clean clothes for him, a clean house, and words of encouragement. His assumption was punctured that warm June day, and his world fell apart. Later, there was reconciliation. She got his attention. From then on he worked at keeping his relationship with her fresh and making her feel important.

Keep Intimacy Fresh

Men seemed prone to decrease their intimacy as the age of their marriage increases. Perhaps it's the nature of the "beast." Be that as it may, we need to take definite, deliberate steps to make sure we stay intimate. Don't fail to kiss your wife good morning. Remember to kiss her good-bye when you leave the house for anything. When riding in the car, be sure and hold her hand, if the baby's car seat doesn't block you. Never fail to put your arms around her and give her a kiss when you walk in the house from work.

I know a couple who have developed a tradition of kissing each other after the blessing for food. It doesn't matter whether it's in a public restaurant or at home, he reaches over and gives her a kiss.

Make sure your lovemaking doesn't get in a routine. It doesn't have to always be at night, always on Tuesdays, or always with the same words.

More women complain about the loss of intimacy in their marriage than anything else. As pointed out in Chapter 1, women are constructed differently from men in temperament, emotions, and mind-set. A man can function fairly well if intimacy goes; a woman cannot live in an emotionally stable way without it, whether she's twenty-three years old or sixty-two.

Occasionally Do the Unenjoyable

All of us husbands have a tough time with this one. There are some things I do not enjoy that my wife enjoys.

I do *not* enjoy putting puzzles together, going to movies, playing card games, window-shopping, or eating out. My wife enjoys all those things. I am learning (slowly) to be a boredom buster by occasionally acquiescing and actually suggesting that we do one of these activities together. It might be good for you to stop right here, men, and write in the margin of this book those things your wife likes to do that you dislike doing, and make an intelligent decision to actually suggest doing one of those things with her. Before you ask her, you might want to have the paramedics' number handy in case she has heart failure!

Go Different Places

Go to a different place to eat with her. When vacation time rolls around, do something different from what you've ever done before. Buy her something different for her anniversary or birthday from anything you've bought in the past. Have you bought perfume for the past nine years? Try clothing. Meet new friends, do different activities. All of this keeps spice in your relationship with her. If you take walks together, drive to a different place, get out, and walk in an area you've never walked in before. Sit at a different place at the table from your usual seat; rearrange your schedule occasionally; sit down together and redefine your goals again. Set new goals.

Work Again and Again at Communication

Again, men are basically not good communicators. They have little or no penchant for details. They tend to assume that their wives know what they're thinking. To keep the sparkle in your marriage, *overkill* with communication. Write notes, love notes, nice notes, but factual notes. Say the same thing the note says. Bend over backward to communicate with your wife. Most monotony is born and bred in the dark waters of "no communication." Men, if your work allows it, call your wife from work at least one time per day, and if possible two or three times. If you have nothing else to communicate to her, tell her you just called to say you love her. Every marriage that has hit the rocks of boredom is a relationship from which communication departed long ago.

Develop a Sense of Humor with Your Wife

Happy is the couple that has learned to laugh together. Learn to laugh *at* yourself. Learn to laugh *with* your wife. Laugh when she laughs at you, and laugh together. A secular counselor once told me that if couples would laugh often with each other, not take themselves so seriously all the time, and lighten up, the sparkle and crispness would stay in their marriage. I know men who can laugh with their business associates, even their secretaries, but they never laugh with their wives; it's all business. Humor not only relieves strained situations but creates an atmosphere of approachability in the marriage.

Keep Your Temple in Good Repair

The Bible says that your body is the temple of the Holy Spirit, or the house where the Holy Spirit lives (see 1 Corinthians 3:16). If that's the case, it ought to be the best-looking house on the street! After people are married for a few years, there is a subtle tendency to "let themselves go" in their appearance. Tummies that were once flat begin to bulge, especially with men.

A special plea to all husbands—keep your bodies physically fit, avoid becoming overweight, keep your hair combed, your face shaved, and seek to look attractive for your wife. This means regular health checkups, dental checkups, and maintaining an overall neat appearance. Men have a tendency to groom for their work, but "let it all hang out" for their wives. Regardless of what your wife does, men, make sure your temple is in good repair, freshly painted, and free of pests.

While jogging, I once saw a couple walking arm-in-arm. They were at least in their mid-sixties, maybe early seventies. They both had a glow on their faces, smiling and glancing at each other. I would say they had been married probably at least forty years, maybe longer. What a picture! No boredom, no monotony, no "business as usual." I thought again to myself, *This is the way God intended it to be.* Make sure you're spending enough time with your wife so that boredom is a word that never enters your family dictionary!

12

BE THE PROVIDER

T he county in which I live recorded almost 9,700 divorces granted in the last year. That means for every working day there were thirty-eight marriages broken. Thirty-eight times, couples divided property, got separate living accommodations, went on a different budget, and in 70 percent of those divorces, children were affected for life. Thirty-eight times every working day last year where I live, couples called it quits in marriage, broke a covenant they made, and began a life, in most cases, of economic hardship, bitterness, some guilt, and in all cases a sense of loneliness to one degree or another.

Many reasons can be given for these breakups. Infidelity, incompatibility, in-laws, finances, and violence, but the bottom line is, most of these people saw marriage as an arrangement that could be slipped into and out of if things didn't work out.

Listen to divorce proceedings, and it will be evident that in almost 60 percent of all divorces, money is a large issue. Behind that are the issues of who supports the family, with how much, and for how long.

I believe Biblically and historically the male has been charged with the primary responsibility of being the breadwinner, the provider, and the protector of the home. After the Fall, the roles assigned to man and woman were fairly clear:

> To the woman [God] said, "I will greatly increase your pains in childbearing; with pain you will give birth to children." (Genesis 3:16)

> To Adam [God] said, ". . . Cursed is the ground because of you; through painful toil you will eat of it all the days of your life." (Genesis 3:17)

We may well call these consequences or results of the fall of man. Whatever we call them, it's clear that one consequence is domestic and is done in the context of the home; the other is vocational, carried out in the context of the field (the workplace).

I fully realize that not all will agree with the thesis of this chapter, but let me state it up front for clarity: *The husband's primary responsibility is to earn the living; the wife's primary responsibility is to be a homemaker.*

Now that I have marked myself, and revealed some old-fashioned values I cherish, let me urge you who *disagree* with that statement to please read on! At least be open to the reasoning behind such a radical view.

When I refer to the working wife, I do not infer that wives who choose to stay home and manage their households don't do any work. The fact is, there is no outside job in the workplace that demands as much energy, creativity, planning, and discipline. But for the sake of definition, I refer to the "working woman" as the one who opts to work for a paycheck outside the home.

The Working Housewife

The working housewife came on the scene suddenly during World War II when help was needed in the defense plants across our nation. When the war ended, couples across America wanted to upgrade their living conditions and saw the two-income family as the way to do it. But the veritable flood of women into the workplace really accelerated in the mid-sixties and seventies, reaching unprecedented proportions in the mid to late eighties. Today, well over half the wives in America work outside the home, including millions with preschool children who are placed in day-care centers. The day-care industry has become one of the fastest growing and most profitable businesses in America today. The current mood today is definitely a "pro-working wife" mood. In the August 24, 1989 issue of *USA Today*, under the "Life" section of that newspaper, the results of a national survey were given that were made for *Self* magazine. In the polling of 1177 women it was found that 59 percent believe the most satisfying life combines careers and kids. Only 7 percent of women want the same lives their moms had — meaning a home and domestic life. The discouraging element of this survey was the indication that 71 percent of full-time homemakers under the age of forty-four say they will go back to work when their kids are in school. What exactly is the pull? What is that mysterious "tug" that pulls wives into the workplace?

To Compensate
for a Husband's Inadequate Income

In a small minority of cases, wives work because the husband has no education or job skills, and the family income must be supplemented just to cover rent, food, transportation, and the fundamental living costs. In some cases, a husband may have become handicapped or sick, and a wife is forced to work so the family can survive.

To Pursue a Career

Some women insist on working, even over the objection of their husbands, because they wish to fulfill themselves with a career. They justify working by saying they have gifts and abilities they should use. My thirty plus years of counseling seem to indicate that marriages in which women work for career reasons have a relatively low survival rate.

To Increase the Standard of Living

Many women work outside the home simply because they and their husbands want a bigger house, a newer car, nicer furniture, more expensive vacations, or more recreational things such as boats, planes, and snowmobiles. In these cases, the family could easily live off the husband's income, but they couldn't have all the toys without the wife working.

Because of Boredom and Lack of Fulfillment

Some wives opt to work because they don't feel fulfilled at home. They are bored with house cleaning, laundry, cooking, and other domestic duties. Rather than seeing their role in the home as a queen in charge of the castle, many wives view housework as demeaning, a drudgery, and boring. As one woman said to me, "I had to leave the house daily anyway and get away from it, so I thought I may as well be bringing home a paycheck while I was away."

Because They Are Forced to Work
by Their Husbands

An increasing number of wives are in the workplace because their husbands have insisted that they work.

They are seen by their husbands as mere consumers if they stay at home. Many men see their wives as a supplemental source of income which will take some pressure off them. Resentment and anger build fast in these marriages, especially in cases where the wife has strong desires to stay at home and care for her children and house. Many women become ill when they are forced out of the home to help bring home the bacon. It seems to always begin by the husband promising that it will only be temporary. Then they are trapped by becoming dependent on the two incomes, so she stays on the job until she becomes ill, or until separation and divorce occur. Some tough it out to the end, but in either case, the husband who pushes his wife into the workplace does her and his family a great disservice.

It's interesting that the Bible speaks of men working in the vineyard, but not women. In the parable of the vineyard in Isaiah 5, the one who tends the vineyard is the man. Three times in that parable, the tender of the vineyard is referred to as "he." In Matthew 20:1, it says that a landowner went out early in the morning to hire "*men*" to work in the vineyard. Many will argue that both references belonged to another time and another culture, and thus do not apply to today. Today it's perfectly acceptable in our culture for wives to work outside the home. Let me respond by saying that we could totally rewrite the Scriptures, leaving out what we feel is "cultural," and we would end up with a map, two fly leaves, and a leather cover! I firmly believe that apart from a few exceptions, God's basic plan is for the husband to be the breadwinner and the wife to be the homemaker.

The Consequences

Men, consider with me some of the consequences of having your wife enter the workplace. Because a track record has been established, we can with confidence state the following consequences.

A Tendency Toward Some Neglect of Marriage and Family

Though certainly not deliberate, and though measures are taken by most working wives for this not to happen, neglect of marriage and family is inevitable. A woman has only so much energy and emotional stamina. It's not just an eight-hour job. It's the two hours getting ready and getting the family ready in the morning, and the hour returning home in rush-hour traffic and trying to wind down that makes somewhere between ten and twelve hours a day, five days a week where her energy is drained by her job. There isn't much energy left for her husband and any children she might have.

A Tendency Toward Independence Develops

Biblically, marriage is leaving and cleaving. A working wife outside the home is prone to lose some dependency she has on her husband and develop independence. After all, she has to be responsible for driving herself to work, buying her own lunch, banking and budgeting her paycheck, and is drawn away from having her husband be the center of her life. Now her job is that center. A spirit of possessiveness sets in. In thirty-three years of counseling couples where the wife left the home to go into the workplace, the common comment by both is: "We don't know how it happened or when, but we just drifted apart into two worlds." Many a husband has lost his wife within a year after she went to work outside the home. No, it doesn't have to happen, but to some degree an unhealthy independence will develop.

Increases the Chances for Affairs

Roger and Sandy had been married only seven years, when they both agreed she would go to work. It was only to be through April when tax season was over. The enjoyment of the extra income, the exhilarating feeling of fulfillment to Sandy, and the fact that the head accountant wanted her to continue on till summer found Sandy going from a temporary job to a full-fledged working wife. Roger came to me in August to say he thought Sandy was having an affair. The "extra work" on Saturday mornings, the two hours late three evenings a week, the fact she was becoming distant and somewhat indifferent to him all raised his antenna of suspicion. He finally confronted her. There was instant blowup, anger, tears, but finally admission that yes, she was seeing her young boss, not only eight hours at work five-and one-half days per week, but after hours as well. She was caught up in a world of excitement with her new attraction.

Roger drove a city bus; she seldom saw him in a three-piece suit. He drove a four-door compact. Her boss wore expensive clothes, was handsome, polite, giving, and drove her to their nightly rendezvous in a new sports car. It all looked so good, but now Sandy had a choice. My counsel was for her to quit her job. She balked! When they were first married, she couldn't wait to quit her job and make a home for Roger. Now it was all different.

This situation had a good ending. Sandy finally saw what had happened to her — she had become another victim of the workplace for wives, and it almost cost her their marriage. This is one of Satan's most subtle trap doors.

She and Roger are happily married today with two children, and she loves being a homemaker. Interestingly enough she has become a crusader for wives to make their careers as homemakers and stay out of the workplace. She sees her highest calling to be what 1 Timothy 5:14 speaks of: "So I counsel younger widows to marry, to have children, to *manage their homes* and to give the enemy no opportunity for slander" (emphasis added). She strongly believes that doesn't just apply to widows, but to all women who opt to marry and raise a family.

Increases the Adverse Effects on Children

A spring issue of *Leadership* magazine stated that 51 percent of all mothers with babies one year old and younger are working outside the home today. This means someone else must mold and shape their child's life and values. It's usually a neighbor, a relative, or the proverbial day-care center. Regardless of who it is, it's not the person God had in mind when He gave you that child. Single moms have little choice at this point, but married women do unless their husbands are forcing them to work.

One working mom who has since quit told me her schedule and the guilt she had in keeping it. She awoke at 5:00 A.M. daily, got herself dressed, awoke her two sleeping preschool boys at 6:00, got them dressed, fed, and packed for the day, strapped them in their car seats, drove at 6:30 to the day care three miles away, unloaded them and their paraphernalia, left them while they both cried every day, and drove twelve miles to her work which took her the better part of forty-five minutes. She began her day's work at 7:50. She left at 5:00, drove the forty-five minutes back to the day care, picked up both kids, drove the three miles home, usually arriving by 6:15 or 6:30. With no time to spend with them, she rushed to prepare dinner for her husband without even changing her clothes; they ate about 7:15, then it was bath time for the boys, then bedtime immediately for them. By 9:00 she was totally exhausted as she tried in vain to carry on a conversation with her husband whom she hadn't seen since 6:15 that morning, usually half asleep.

Who suffers? Everyone in the family, but especially the kids. Someone else will watch them take their first step. Someone else will potty train them. Someone else will hear one of them say his first word. Someone else will hold them when they fall and cry. Someone else will detect the diaper rash or the measles or the chickenpox or a runny nose. For almost ten hours, five days a week, someone else is raising them, changing them, cuddling them, and speaking to them.

No position, no amount of recognition, no paycheck could be big enough to make that worth it. Do you think it's easier if they're older? I have observed this: latchkey kids in America are much more prone to get into trouble, smoke pot, drink booze, have sex, and be adversely influenced by neighbor kids than kids whose moms are not out in the workplace. They're sick more often, fail in school more often, and develop personality idiosyncrasies more readily than do kids whose moms opt to stay home. More respect is lost for both parents when moms are gone nine hours each day. Discipline becomes harder and harder as they get older and older.

Increases Opportunities to Argue over Money

Working moms become extremely protective and jealous over their paychecks. Few, with compliance, bring them home, endorse them, and put them in the family fund. The truth is that hassles develop, arguments ensue, and funds in the marriage become "mine" and "yours." Most of this is avoided when husbands decide to be the only breadwinner in the family.

With the help of an accountant, I recently did a breakdown of the normal expenses incurred when a wife works outside the home (see Table 1). There may be a few variations here and there, but basically this is very accurate, pointing out that from an economic standpoint, it doesn't pay for a wife to work outside the home. This study was done in the community where I live, so costs and prices will reflect my local economy. This is based on a job where a wife earns three hundred dollars per week, has two preschool children that must be cared for at a day-care center, and works five days per week. These items are purchased by both homemakers and working mothers. The expenses show the added calculated costs incurred by a working mother.

Table 1 Weekly Expenses, Income, and Profit for a Working Wife	
Expenses	
Tithe (if she's a Christian)	$30
Taxes	$27
Transportation	$20 (gas,oil, tires,etc)
Lunch	$15 (at work and from home)
Carry-Outs for Dinner	$20 (times too tired to cook)
Additional Clothes	$15 (hose, shoes, jewelry)
Feel She Owes to Self	$12 (personal treats she "deserves")
Child Care	$144 (day care; 2 kids)
Gifts (at workplace)	$6 (birthdays,weddings, etc.)
Total	$289
Income	
Total	$300
Profit (Income Minus Expenses)	
Total	$11

What isn't calculated in the above table is the extremely high cost of her being an absent wife and mom.

Sure, she may find a cheaper day care, but not much cheaper; yes, she may lower her transportation costs; true, she could leave off the tithe. She may cut here and there, but still the net take-home-and-keep is pretty low. If the above has any accuracy, husbands would avoid potential grief by giving their wives an extra eleven dollars each week.

To be sure, there are exceptions, as previously mentioned, where at least temporarily, wives find it necessary to work outside the home. Also, the consequences mentioned are greatly lessened as children get into the mid-teen years and don't require constant supervision. The effects are also lessened among "empty-nesters" who both agree to the wife working outside the home. But by and large, men, as the heads of households, need to earn the living for the family.

Many have argued, "But what about the godly woman of Proverbs 31?" If you read that chapter carefully, you'll discover that most, if not all, that she does is in the context of the home. She brings her husband good, not harm; she sews, she cooks, she plants a garden, and her trading that is profitable probably has to do with products she has produced at home. In saying she opens her arms to the poor probably means she opens her house up to them. Verse 22 of that chapter says she makes coverings for her bed. It's pretty hard to decorate your home yourself and work forty hours a week somewhere else. I think the key verse in that chapter that nails down her domestic excellence is verse 27: "She watches over the affairs of her household and does not eat the bread of idleness."

It's no wonder her children rise up and call her blessed. They don't rise up and congratulate her because she helped the company win the seven-million-dollar contract; they simply rise up and call her blessed.

Husbands, be the provider. Protect your wife. Don't release her from your covering of protection so she's thrown to the wolves in the workplace. No amount of extra income she can bring home can ever pay for the long-term damage done by full-time employment outside the home.

13

MARRIAGE IS
FOR KEEPS

S omeone saw a true sign of the times in a Holly-
wood jewelry store. It was a small sign that read:
"We Rent Wedding Rings."

It is the age of the disposable, the cartridge, the
throwaway, the temporary. One couple, reflecting the
mood of the times in marriage, had these words in-
serted in their ceremony: "Nothing is forever. . . . We
both this day promise to be understanding if the other
desires to end this federation of marriage."

Whether it's said or not, it happens. One out of
every two marriages that takes place will be shattered
in less than eight years. Perhaps it's reflective of the
philosophy of our time that commitments are made to
be broken, contracts consummated to become null and
void, and agreements made to be undone. When I was
a boy, I saw my father shake hands with a man con-

cerning the sale of a very small piece of property in our backyard. No written contracts, no attorneys, no affidavits, no notary public, they simply shook hands. One man agreed to pay my dad four hundred dollars, and my dad believed him. It was a deal between two men whose word was as sure as the sunrise the next day. Sure enough, within the year, the man had paid the whole amount of money. Those days exist only in the annals of history now. Lawsuits abound today between parties even where papers were signed, collateral put up, and covenants were agreed to.

As the head of the family, a husband has a great responsibility to do many things in the marriage. None, however, is greater than being the one who sees that the contract is never broken.

God conceived marriage. He drew its guidelines on His master drawing board. Like the skilled architect He is, He ordained that marriage be the first and most important institution He would ever create.

There are two words that reflect God's will for marriage: *unity* and *permanence.* In all the shuffle of modern thinking, it is precisely those two words that have been misplaced.

Remember Adam exclaimed, "This is now bone of my bones and flesh of my flesh" (Genesis 2:23). Husbands today forget, but that is a very significant statement. It means that the raw material God used to form woman came directly from man. She is made of the same "stuff" as man.

Then God said, "For this reason a man will leave his father and mother and be united to his wife, and they will become one flesh" (Genesis 2:24). Unity! There is a leaving and a cleaving. Adam had no earthly parents to leave, yet God still spoke of it to get across the absolute essentialness of the man cutting all ties he had heretofore and establishing the tie to his wife. We're talking about a special divine bonding here. There really is not an adequate Hebrew word for *united.* Older versions used the words *cleave to his wife.* Some use *joined to his wife.* It's not, as some have suggested, some kind of divine "supergluing" process. It's not the attaching of one object to another. Rivets can come out of metal, and planes fall from the sky. Glue doesn't hold forever. Staples rust and lose their strength. No, it's something much closer and more intimate. It's a blending that creates something new that hasn't existed before and that is not designed to ever be unmixed to its original two parts.

For example, you can take a quart of white paint and a quart of red paint and pour them into a gallon container. Once mixed, you have one-half gallon of pink paint. Suppose someone says after you've mixed them, "I don't want pink after all, but red and white on the walls." Sorry, too late, you cannot separate the two paints. I believe that's the kind of unity God is talking about when He says the two have become one flesh. Yes, marriage is a forfeiture of rights to a great degree, and people who don't want that should not even think of getting married. It's no wonder God said, "I hate divorce" (Malachi 2:16). It leaves both parties less than what they were when married. You can't unscramble an egg. Just try!

Next, there is *permanence.* God never intended the dissolution of any marriage. The Pharisees once asked Jesus if it were lawful to divorce one's wife for any reason. What they really wanted to know was did He subscribe to the teaching of Rabbi Hillel who taught a very liberal position on divorce and remarriage. Jesus' answer to them takes them back to God's original intention:

> "Haven't you read," he replied, "that at the beginning the Creator 'made them male and female,' and said, 'For this reason a man will leave his father and mother and be united to his wife, and the two will become one flesh'? So they are no longer two, but one. Therefore what God has joined together, let man not separate." (Matthew 19:4-6)

Notice that Jesus didn't reference the current prevailing mood of divorce and remarriage, which like today, had become very loose. He referenced marriage as God intended it to be.

The Pharisees tried to entangle Jesus by saying that Moses commanded a man to give his wife a certificate of divorce and send her away. Jesus' answer is golden. It holds the key to what ought to be preached about marriage today: "Jesus replied, 'Moses *permitted* you to divorce your wives because your hearts were hard.

But it was not this way from the beginning'" (Matthew 19:8, emphasis added).

He silenced them by telling them that they were buying into a practice that came about because of hard hearts, but that this wasn't God's best and original plan. Moses was saying, if you're going to divorce and go against God's will, don't forget the paperwork! Moses never recommended divorce, nor did he suggest it, urge it, or condone it. He *permitted* it in order to regulate it. So for man to entertain the idea of divorce today is to consider something that came about by man's sin rather than to stay with God's original plan that says man is not to separate what God has put together.

Marriage is until death. But surely someone reading this chapter will say, "But wait, doesn't the Bible have God-authorized grounds for divorce?" The answer is yes. It's called adultery. But remember this: because marriage is a three-way covenant between God, man, and woman, the obligation to forgive the adulterer takes precedence over the *right* to divorce. (See Chapter 7.)

The fact is, marriage is till *death* do us part, not till debt or disagreement or derogatory words do us part.

I fully believe that because the man has been ordained by God to be the head of the marriage, it is primarily up to him to maintain a divorce-free relationship. Men, don't even allow the word *divorce* to be spoken in your house. Regardless of the hard times, the lost feelings, the gigantic challenges — *stay married.* It's God's will.

Our thesis all along has been this: The husband is *ultimately* responsible for the success of the marriage. That doesn't mean wives don't work at marriage. It doesn't mean that wives are not to share the credit or the blame for the ups and downs of holy marriage. It *does* mean, however, that the husband has been called by God to be the key force in maintaining and cultivating the marriage. The best way to do this is by fervent prayer. I close with what I've called "The Prayer of Every Husband":

O Lord, I lift to you the most prized possession of my life — my dear wife. Forgive me, Lord, for assuming too much, forgive the foolishness of taking her for granted. Redeem me, O Lord, from the sin of insensitivity and apathy. Deliver me, O Lord, from the failure to cherish her as the apple of my eye, the most prized possession of my life, from listening but not hearing, from being miles away while I'm with her at home. Purge me, O Lord, from the busyness that consumes my attention, leaving none for her. Cleanse me, O God, of the cutting and painful remarks I carelessly make, and the dozens of times I don't respond at all because my head is in a fog!

Lord, fill my mouth with praise for her instead of complaints, with positive words instead of negative, with stroking words instead of grating, with smooth words instead of harsh ones.

Lord, this is my wife. May there be no time in her life that her spirit is injured by what I say or don't say or wrongly say. Show me how to cherish her, lift her, exalt her, placing and leaving her at the right level on my scale of priorities. Show me how to feed and nurture her, how to build her up, how to alleviate her fears, banish her doubts, scatter her gloom, wipe her tears, bandage her hurts, and how to pour oil on her wounds in such a way that she knows she's tops on my list. Teach me how to put her first, raise her high, make her shine, protect her always, and love her like Christ loved the church.

Lord, this is my wife You've created for me. May I never use her, but love her; may I never thwart her, but encourage her; may I never intimidate her, but honor her; may I never smother her, but grant her freedom. Let my love cover her sins, my generosity blanket her being, my leadership give her confidence. When our trek is over, Lord, may she look back and say, "It was a good journey with a good man, and there are no regrets." Amen.

ABOUT THE AUTHOR

Dr. Bob Moorehead has been the pastor of Overlake Christian Church in Kirkland, Washington for twenty years. He has seen the church grow from ninety people to a congregation of six thousand today. His very active and successful ministry there emphasizes counseling, teaching, and evangelism.

Dr. Moorehead holds a Ph.D. from California School of Theology as well as an undergraduate degree from Phillips University and a Bachelor of Divinity degree from The Graduate Seminary. He is the author of three other books: *Free at Last* (College Press), *The Growth Factor* (College Press), and *The Marriage Repair Kit* (Wolgemuth and Hyatt).

Bob and his wife, Glenita, live in Kirkland, Washington. They have three grown children: Darla, Tammi, and Jeff.

The typeface for the text of this book is *Times Roman*. In 1930, typographer Stanley Morison joined the staff of *The Times* (London) to supervise design of a typeface for the reformatting of this renowned English daily. Morison had overseen type-library reforms at Cambridge University Press in 1925, but this new task would prove a formidable challenge despite a decade of experience in paleography, calligraphy, and typography. *Times New Roman* was credited as coming from Morison's original pencil renderings in the first years of the 1930s, but the typeface went through numerous changes under the scrutiny of a critical committee of dissatisfied *Times* staffers and editors. The resulting typeface, *Times Roman*, has been called the most used, most successful typeface of this century. The design is of enduring value to English and American printers and publishers, who choose the typeface for its readability and economy when run on today's high-speed presses.

Substantive Editing:
Michael Hyatt

Copy Editing:
Susan Kirby

Cover Design:
Steve Diggs & Friends
Nashville, Tennessee

Page Composition:
Xerox Ventura Publisher
Printware 720 IQ Laser Printer

Printing and Binding:
Ringier America
Olathe, Kansas